Renew Our Hearts
A Siddur for Shabbat Day

חדש לבבנו

Renew Our Hearts: A Siddur for Shabbat Day. Copyright © 2023 by Bayit: Building Jewish. All rights reserved. No part of this book may be used or reproduced in any manner whatsoever without written permission except in the case of brief quotations embodied in critical articles and reviews.

Sources of the original translations and poems in this volume can be found on page 158, which constitutes an extension of this copyright page.

Published by Ben Yehuda Press
122 Ayers Court #1B
Teaneck, NJ 07666
http://www.BenYehudaPress.com

To subscribe to our monthly book club and support independent Jewish publishing, visit https://www.patreon.com/BenYehudaPress.

Ben Yehuda Press books may be purchased at a discount by synagogues, book clubs, and other institutions buying in bulk. For information, please email markets@BenYehudaPress.com.

ISBN13 978-1-953829-28-3 pb
978-1-953829-29-0 hc
978-1-953829-68-9 pb - large print
978-1-953829-69-6 hc - large print

22 23 24 / 8 7 6 5 4 3   20240917

For all the builders
co-creating the Judaism our world needs
for today and tomorrow.

תלמידי חכמים מרבים שלום בעולם שנאמר
וכל בניך למודי ה' ורב שלום בניך
אל תקרי בניך אלא בוניך

"Students of the wise increase shalom (peace, completeness) in the world,
as it is said (Isaiah 54:13):
'[Thus] all your children will be taught of God.'
Don't read it as 'your children' (*banayich*) but as 'your builders' (*bonayich*)."

(Brachot 64a)

Contents

Openings — 1
- *Hareini M'kabeil Alai:* Here I Take Upon Myself — 1
- *Esa Einai:* I Lift My Eyes Up — 1
- Sanctuary — 2
- Holy Space — 2

Morning Blessings — 3
- *Modeh Ani:* Blessing for Gratitude — 3
- Meditation on Possibilities — 3
- Putting on Tallit — 4
- *Mah Tovu:* How Lovely Are Your Tents! — 5
- *Elohai Neshama*: Blessing for the Soul — 6
- *Asher Yatzar*: Blessing for the Body — 7
- A Prayer in Unlikely Places — 8
- Blessings for Each Day — 9

Psukei D'Zimra: Psalms of Praise — 11
- *Baruch She•amar:* Blessed is the One Who Speaks — 11
    - Short *Baruch She•amar* Chant — 11
    - Full text *Baruch She•amar* — 12
- From Psalm 30 — 13
- Mourner's *Kaddish* — 13
- from Psalm 92 — 15
- *Ashrei* — 16
    - Full-Text *Ashrei* — 18
    - Renewed *Ashrei* — 19
- Psalm 136 / *Ki L'Olam Chasdo* — 20
- Body Hodu (Psalm 136) — 22
- Psalm 148 — 23
- Psalm 150 — 24
- Give Praise — 24
- From *Nishmat Kol Chai:* The Breath of All Life — 25
- *Nishmat* — 26
- *Yishtabach*: Blessing Ending *Psukei D'Zimrah* — 28
- Your Name Be Praised — 29
- The *Kaddish*: A Door — 30
- *Chatzi Kaddish* — 30

The Shema & Her Blessings — 31

Bar'chu / Call to Prayer	31
Yotzer Or / Blessing for Light	31
Yotzer Or Chant	31
Full text *Yotzer Or*	32
Yotzer Or / Blessing for Light	34
Good (*Yotzer Or*)	37
Ahavah Rabbah / Blessing for Love (and Torah)	38
Ahavah Rabbah Chant (*Lach Amar Libi*, from Psalm 27)	38
Full text *Ahavah Rabbah*	38
More Love (Shaker *Ahavah Rabbah*)	40
So much (*Ahavah Rabbah*)	41
Shema	42
Listen Up Y'all / An interpretive version of וְהָיָה אִם שָׁמֹעַ	54
Ge·ulah / Blessing for Redemption	47
Short *Ge·ulah* Chant	47
Full Text *Ge·ulah*	48
The Water is Wide	51
Journey	53

Amidah — 55

Full Text *Amidah*	55
Avot V'imahot / Ancestors	55
Gevurot / Strength	56
Kidushat HaShem Option I / Sanctification of God's Name	58
Kidushat HaShem Option II / Sanctification of God's Name	60
Kidushat HaYom Shel Shacharit / Blessing the Day - Morning Service	62
Kidushat HaYom Shel Mincha / Blessing the Day - Afternoon Service	63
Kidushat HaYom / Blessing the Day continued - Morning & Afternoon	64
On Rosh Chodesh, and on the intermediate days of festivals:	65
On Chanukah and Purim:	68
Elohai N'tzor	72
Sanctuary	73
The *Kaddish*: A Door	73
Chatzi Kaddish / Half Kaddish	74

Torah Service — 75

Blessing before Torah	77
Blessing after Torah	77
Mi Shebeirach / Prayer for Healing	78
Haftarah	80
Blessing Before the Haftarah	80
Blessings After the Haftarah	80
Returning the Torah to the Ark	82
Chatzi Kaddish / Half Kaddish	83

Musaf: "Extra" — 84

Questions for Silent Contemplation	84
Kedushat HaYom: The Holiness of This Day (for Shabbat Musaf)	85
Kedushah Keter: The Crown	85
Yismechu: Rejoice	86
Offering: What We Do For Love	86
Tikanta Shabbat: You Instituted Shabbat...	87
Descending Through the Alphabet	87
Psalm 29: Chant	88
Psalm 29: Full-text	89
Chatzi Kaddish / Half Kaddish	90
Ein k'Eloheinu	91
Non komo muestro Dyo	92

(Morning Service) Closings — 93

Aleinu	93
Aleinu Chants	93
Full Text *Aleinu*	94
Mourner's *Kaddish*	98
Songs	100
Yigdal	100
Adon Olam	102
Home	104

Mincha: Afternoon Offering — 106

Ashrei — 107
Uva L'Tzion: A Prayer for Redemption — 107
Chatzi Kaddish — 110
Torah — 111
Blessing before Torah — 112
Blessing after Torah — 112
Shabbat Afternoon *Amidah* — 113
Contemplative *Amidah* — 113
Imahot v'Avot / Ancestors — 113

Maariv / Evening Prayer — 115

Barchu — Call to Prayer — 115
V'Hu Rachum / The Merciful One — 115
Maariv Aravim: Who Evens the Evenings — 116
Ahavat Olam: Unending Love — 117
Sh'ma: Oneness — 119
G'ulah: Redemption — 122
Hashkiveinu: Shelter of Peace — 125
from *Baruch* יהוה *L'Olam*: Blessed is the One Forever — 126
The *Kaddish*: A Door — 126
Chatzi Kaddish / Half Kaddish — 127
Weekday *Amidah* — 128
    Contemplative *Amidah* — 128
    Full Text *Amidah* — 133
The Kaddish: A Door — 149
Kaddish Shaleim — 149
Aleinu: Od Yavo Shalom — 151
Mourner's *Kaddish* — 152

Havdalah — 155

Sources and Permissions — 158

I OPENINGS

> ### Ways of Speaking to the One
>
> God has many names in Jewish tradition, among them *Elohim* (God), יהוה (or *YHVH*: an untranslatable permutation of the verb "to be"), *Havayah* (also a permutation of the verb "to be"), *Ahavah* (Love), *Adonai* (Lord), *Shechinah* (indwelling, feminine Presence), *Ein Hachayim* (Source of Life), *Melech* (King), *Malkah* (Queen), *Ruach* (Breath of Life), *Avinu* (Our Father), *Imeinu* (Our Mother), Beloved, Friend, Creator, Wellspring, Source, Hidden One, Merciful One, Judge, Parent, and more. Use whatever Names best enable you to relate to the Divine.
>
> We've chosen not to translate or transliterate the ancient name יהוה. Its untranslatability points us beyond all words. Jewish tradition teaches that our Creator is beyond language: our words can only approach the Infinite. May our linguistic choices remind us that our names are only substitutes, and that our Source is beyond any words we can speak.

Openings

Hareini M'kabeil Alai: Here I Take Upon Myself

הֲרֵינִי מְקַבֵּל עָלַי Hareini m'kabel alai
אֶת מִצְוַת הַבּוֹרֵא Et mitzvat haborei
וְאָהַבְתָּ לְרֵעֲךָ כָּמוֹךָ, V'ahavta l're·acha kamocha
לְרֵעֲךָ כָּמוֹךָ. L're·acha kamocha.

Here I take upon myself
The *mitzvah* of my Creator:
Love your neighbor as yourself,
Your neighbor as yourself.

Esa Einai: I Lift My Eyes Up

אֶשָּׂא עֵינַי אֶל הֶהָרִים. Esa einai el heharim.
מֵאַיִן יָבֹא עֶזְרִי? Mei·ayin yavo ezri?
עֶזְרִי מֵעִם יהוה, Ezri mei·im יהוה,
עֹשֵׂה שָׁמַיִם וָאָרֶץ. oseh shamayim va·aretz.

I lift my eyes up to the mountains: from where comes my help?
My help is from the Holy Blessed One, creator of the heavens and the earth.

(From Psalm 121)

Sanctuary

וְעָשׂוּ לִי מִקְדָּשׁ וְשָׁכַנְתִּי בְּתוֹכָם V'asu li mikdash v'shachanti b'tocham
וַאֲנַחְנוּ נְבָרֵךְ יָהּ מֵעַתָּה וְעַד עוֹלָם! Va·anachnu n'vareich Yah mei·ata v'ad olam!

O Lord, prepare me to be a sanctuary: pure and holy, tried and true
And in thanksgiving I'll be a living sanctuary for You!

Holy Space

When we pray together, our sense of community creates holiness.
When we gather together as a community, we create holy space.
When we sing together, our voices lift spirit and soul.
When we rejoice together in song, we create holy music.
When we study together, our struggle to find meaning helps us find wholeness.
When we learn together, we know what it is to stretch into holiness.
When we perform acts of *tikkun olam* together,
our healing works to make the world whole.
When we work together to repair the whole, we know that we create holiness.
When we come together for study, prayer, song and story, we are a holy community.
When we come together, we create holy space.

(Susan R. Schorr)

Morning Blessings

Modeh Ani: Blessing for Gratitude

מוֹדֶה/מוֹדָה/מוֹדֶת* אֲנִי לְפָנֶיךָ, Modeh/modah/modet* ani l'fanecha,
מֶלֶךְ חַי וְקַיָּם, melech chai v'kayam,
שֶׁהֶחֱזַרְתָּ בִּי נִשְׁמָתִי shehechezarta bi nishmati
בְּחֶמְלָה רַבָּה אֱמוּנָתֶךָ! b'chemlah. Raba emunatecha.

I am grateful before You,
living and enduring God:
You have restored my soul to me.
Great is Your faithfulness!

**Hebrew is a gendered language; traditionally men say* מוֹדֶה *modeh and women say* מוֹדָה *modah; a new nonbinary form is* מוֹדֶת *modet.*

Meditation on Possibilities

Each early morning,
my eyes open to a streaky sunrise.
The calls of stirring birds eager
to start their busy seeking
inspirit my newly-returned soul.

Creator of every mysterious dawn,
poised in this pregnant moment,
preparing
to unfurl the fabric of the coming day,

You send these signs as reminders:
Savor each unmerited gift of awakening.
Arise in awe.
In gratitude, step into the everyday:
marvels await.

(Rabbi Janet Madden)

Putting on Tallit

בָּרְכִי נַפְשִׁי אֶת יהוה, Barchi nafshi et יהוה,
יהוה אֱלֹהַי גָּדַלְתָּ מְּאֹד. יהוה Elohai gadalta me·od.
הוֹד וְהָדָר לָבָשְׁתָּ, עֹטֶה אוֹר כַּשַּׂלְמָה. Hod vehadar lavashta, oteh or k'salmah.
נוֹטֶה שָׁמַיִם כַּיְרִיעָה. Noteh shamayim k'yeri·ah.

בָּרוּךְ אַתָּה יהוה Baruch atah יהוה
אֱלֹהֵינוּ מֶלֶךְ הָעוֹלָם Eloheinu melech ha·olam
אֲשֶׁר קִדְּשָׁנוּ בְּמִצְוֹתָיו וְצִוָּנוּ asher kid'shanu b'mitsvotav v'tzivanu
לְהִתְעַטֵּף בַּצִּיצִית. l'hitateif batzitzit.

Bless יהוה, my soul!
יהוה, my God, You are very great.
You are dressed in glory and splendor,
Wearing light like a gown.
You spread out the heavens like a cloth.

Blessed are You, יהוה our God, source of all being:
You make us holy in connecting-command
and enjoin us to wrap ourselves with tzitzit.

Mah Tovu: How Lovely Are Your Tents!

מַה טֹּבוּ אֹהָלֶיךָ יַעֲקֹב, Mah tovu ohalecha Ya·akov,
מִשְׁכְּנֹתֶיךָ יִשְׂרָאֵל. mishk'notecha Yisra·el.

וַאֲנִי בְּרֹב חַסְדְּךָ אָבוֹא בֵיתֶךָ, Va·ani b'rov chasdecha avo veitecha,
אֶשְׁתַּחֲוֶה אֶל הֵיכַל קָדְשְׁךָ eshtachaveh el heichal kodsh'cha
בְּיִרְאָתֶךָ. b'yiratecha.

יהוה אָהַבְתִּי מְעוֹן בֵּיתֶךָ, יהוה ahavti me·on beitecha,
וּמְקוֹם מִשְׁכַּן כְּבוֹדֶךָ. um'kom mishkan k'vodecha.

וַאֲנִי אֶשְׁתַּחֲוֶה וְאֶכְרָעָה, Va·ani eshtachaveh ve·echra·ah,
אֶבְרְכָה לִפְנֵי יהוה עֹשִׂי. evrechah lifnei יהוה osi.

וַאֲנִי, תְפִלָּתִי לְךָ יהוה, עֵת רָצוֹן, Va·ani tefilati l'cha יהוה eit ratzon,
אֱלֹהִים בְּרָב חַסְדֶּךָ, Elohim b'rov chasdecha,
עֲנֵנִי בֶּאֱמֶת יִשְׁעֶךָ. aneini b'emet yishecha.

How lovely are your tents, O Jacob;
your dwellings, O Israel.

I enter Your house, filled with Your overflowing love.
I bow down to Your holy Temple in awe.

יהוה, how much do I love Your house,
the place where Your glory dwells.

I bow low and prostrate myself,
blessing יהוה, my maker.

I offer this prayer at this moment to You, יהוה.
God, abundant in love, answer me with Your redemption!

Elohai Neshama: Blessing for the Soul

אֱלֹהַי, נְשָׁמָה שֶׁנָּתַתָּ בִּי טְהוֹרָה הִיא.   Elohai neshamah shenatata bi t'horah hi.

אַתָּה בְרָאתָהּ, אַתָּה יְצַרְתָּהּ,   Atah v'ratah atah y'tzartah
אַתָּה נְפַחְתָּהּ בִּי,   atah n'fachtah bi
וְאַתָּה מְשַׁמְּרָהּ בְּקִרְבִּי,   v'atah m'sham'rah b'kirbi
וְאַתָּה עָתִיד לִטְּלָהּ מִמֶּנִּי,   v'atah atid lit'lah mimeni
וּלְהַחֲזִירָהּ בִּי לֶעָתִיד לָבוֹא.   ul'hachazirah bi l'atid lavo.
כָּל זְמַן שֶׁהַנְּשָׁמָה בְקִרְבִּי,   Kol z'man shehan'shamah v'kirbi
מוֹדֶה/מוֹדָה/מוֹדֶת* אֲנִי לְפָנֶיךָ,   Modeh/modah/modet* ani l'fanecha
יהוה אֱלֹהַי וֵאלֹהֵי אֲבוֹתַי וְאִמּוֹתַי,   יהוה Elohai v'Elohei avotai ve-imotai
רִבּוֹן כָּל הַמַּעֲשִׂים, אֲדוֹן כָּל הַנְּשָׁמוֹת.   ribon kol hama·asim adon kol han'shamot.
בָּרוּךְ אַתָּה יהוה,   Baruch atah יהוה
הַמַּחֲזִיר נְשָׁמוֹת לִפְגָרִים מֵתִים.   hamachazir n'shamot lifgarim meitim.

My God ✦ the soul ✦ that You breathed in me ✦ pure is she!

You created it, You formed it, You breathed it into me,
You protect it within me, and, someday,
You will take it from me to return it in a time beyond time.
As long as this soul is within me I shall thank You,
יהוה my God and God of my ancestors, author of every action,
creator of every soul.
Blessed are You, יהוה,
who protects our souls beyond life and death.

*Hebrew is a gendered language; traditionally men say מוֹדֶה *modeh* and women say מוֹדָה *modah*; a new nonbinary form is מוֹדֶת *modet*.

Asher Yatzar: Blessing for the Body

בָּרוּךְ אַתָּה יהוה	Baruch atah יהוה
אֱלֹהֵינוּ מֶלֶךְ הָעוֹלָם,	Eloheinu melech ha·olam,
אֲשֶׁר יָצַר אֶת הָאָדָם בְּחָכְמָה,	asher yatzar et ha·adam b'chochmah
וּבָרָא בוֹ נְקָבִים נְקָבִים,	u'vara vo n'kavim n'kavim
חֲלוּלִים חֲלוּלִים,	chalulim chalulim.
גָּלוּי וְיָדוּעַ לִפְנֵי כִסֵּא כְבוֹדֶךָ	Galui v'yadua lifnei chisei ch'vodecha
שֶׁאִם יִפָּתֵחַ אֶחָד מֵהֶם,	she·im yipate·ach echad meihem
אוֹ יִסָּתֵם אֶחָד מֵהֶם,	o-yisateim echad meihem,
אִי אֶפְשַׁר לְהִתְקַיֵּם	i efshar l'hitkayeim
וְלַעֲמוֹד לְפָנֶיךָ.	v'la·amod l'fanecha.
בָּרוּךְ אַתָּה יהוה,	Baruch atah יהוה
רוֹפֵא כָל בָּשָׂר וּמַפְלִיא לַעֲשׂוֹת.	rofei chol basar umafli la·asot.

Blessed are You, יהוה our God, source of all being,
Who formed the human body with wisdom
and Who placed within us
a miraculous combination of organs and arteries, tissues and sinews.
Clearly, we would not be able to praise Your miracles
were it not for the miracle within us.
Blessed are You, יהוה, healer of all flesh and worker of miracles.

A Prayer in Unlikely Places

In places that seem closed to prayer
And spaces too open to hardship

May openings and closings be for good
For without them I could not stand

To glorify the starry sky
And praise the mother sea.

May openings and closings be for good
For without them I could not stand

To sway in mid-summer sultry breeze
Or dare to dance in mid-winter twilight.

May openings and closings be for good
For without them I could not stand

To bless the healer and the healing, the
Flow of miracles both seen and unseen.

בָּרוּךְ אַתָּה יהוה, Baruch Atah יהוה,
רוֹפֵא כָל בָּשָׂר וּמַפְלִיא לַעֲשׂוֹת. rofei chol basar umafli la·asot.

Blessed are You, Miraculous One, Healer of all flesh, doing wonders.

(Rabbi David Evan Markus)

Blessings for Each Day

בָּרוּךְ אַתָּה יהוה Baruch atah יהוה,
אֱלֹהֵינוּ מֶלֶךְ הָעוֹלָם. Eloheinu melech ha·olam.

Blessed are You, יהוה our God, Source of all being:

OR

בְּרוּכָה אַתְּ יָהּ Brucha at Yah
שְׁכִינָה אֱלָתֵנוּ רוּחַ הָעוֹלָם. Shechinah Elateinu ruach ha·olam.

Blessed are You, Shechinah, our God, breath of life:

אֲשֶׁר נָתַן לַשֶּׂכְוִי בִינָה…. ….asher natan l'sechvi vinah
לְהַבְחִין בֵּין יוֹם וּבֵין לָיְלָה. l'havchin bein yom uvein laila.

…Who gives us discernment to tell day from night;

שֶׁעָשַׂנִי יִשְׂרָאֵל…. ….she·asani Yisra·el.

… Who made me a Jew;

שֶׁעָשַׂנִי בֶּן/בַּת/בֶּת* חוֹרִין…. ….she·asani ben/bat/bet* chorin.

… Who made me free;

שֶׁעָשַׂנִי בְּצַלְמוֹ/בְּצַלְמָהּ…. ….she·asani b'tzalmo/b'tzalmah.

… Who made me in Your image;

פּוֹקֵחַ עִוְרִים…. ….poke·ach ivrim.

… Who opens the eyes of the blind;

מַלְבִּישׁ עֲרֻמִּים…. ….malbish arumim.

… Who clothes the naked;

---

*Hebrew is a gendered language; traditionally men say בֶּן ben and women say בַּת bat; a new nonbinary form is בֶּת bet.

מַתִּיר אֲסוּרִים... ...matir asurim.

... Who frees the captive;

זוֹקֵף כְּפוּפִים... ...zokeif kefufim.

... Who straightens the bent;

רוֹקַע הָאָרֶץ עַל הַמָּיִם... ...roka ha·aretz al ha-mayim.

... Who stretches the earth over the waters;

שֶׁעָשָׂה לִי כָּל צָרְכִּי... ...she·asa li kol tzorki.

... Who gives me all I need;

הַמֵּכִין מִצְעֲדֵי גָבֶר... ...hamechin mitzadei gaver.

... Who strengthens our steps;

אוֹזֵר יִשְׂרָאֵל בִּגְבוּרָה... ...ozer Yisra·el big'vurah.

... Who enfolds Israel in strength;

עוֹטֵר יִשְׂרָאֵל בְּתִפְאָרָה... ...oter Yisra·el b'tifarah.

... Who crowns Israel in splendor;

הַנּוֹתֵן לַיָּעֵף כֹּחַ... ...hanotein laya·ef ko·ach.

... Who gives strength to the weary;

הַמַּעֲבִיר שֵׁנָה מֵעֵינַי... ...hame·avir sheina mei·einai
וּתְנוּמָה מֵעַפְעַפָּי.   utnumah meafapai.

... Who wipes sleep from the eyes, and slumber from the eyelids;

(*You may add more blessings in your own words.*)

...For whatever unspoken blessings are in our hearts.

Psukei D'Zimra: Psalms of Praise

Baruch She·amar: Blessed is the One Who Speaks

Short Baruch She·amar Chant

בָּרוּךְ הוּא, בָּרוּךְ שְׁמוֹ 1) Baruch hu, baruch shemo
בְּרוּכָה הִיא, בָּרוּךְ שְׁמָהּ.   Brucha hi, baruch shema.

בָּרוּךְ שֶׁאָמַר 2) Baruch she·amar
וְהָיָה הָעוֹלָם.   v'haya ha·olam.

(Blessed is He, blessed is His Name; Blessed is She, blessed is Her Name. Blessed is the One who speaks and the world comes into being!)

(Calligraphy by Michel D'Anastasio.)

Full text Baruch She·amar

בָּרוּךְ שֶׁאָמַר	Baruch she·amar
וְהָיָה הָעוֹלָם, בָּרוּךְ הוּא,	vehaya ha·olam. Baruch hu.
בָּרוּךְ עֹשֶׂה בְרֵאשִׁית,	Baruch oseh v'reishit.
בָּרוּךְ אוֹמֵר וְעֹשֶׂה,	Baruch omeir v'oseh.
בָּרוּךְ גּוֹזֵר וּמְקַיֵּם,	Baruch gozeir um'kayeim.
בָּרוּךְ מְרַחֵם עַל הָאָרֶץ,	Baruch m'racheim al ha·aretz.
בָּרוּךְ מְרַחֵם עַל הַבְּרִיּוֹת,	Baruch m'racheim al habriot.
בָּרוּךְ מְשַׁלֵּם שָׂכָר טוֹב לִירֵאָיו,	Baruch m'shaleim sachar tov lirei·av.
בָּרוּךְ חַי לָעַד וְקַיָּם לָנֶצַח,	Baruch chai la·ad v'kayam lanetzach.
בָּרוּךְ פּוֹדֶה וּמַצִּיל, בָּרוּךְ שְׁמוֹ.	Baruch podeh umatzil, baruch shemo.

Blessed is the One who speaks
and the universe comes into being.
Blessed is the One!
Blessed is the One whose thought sustains the world's existence.
Blessed is the One whose mercy is the womb of the world.
Blessed is the One who rewards!
Blessed is the One who is eternal!
Blessed is the One who saves!
Blessed is the Name!

בָּרוּךְ אַתָּה יהוה אֱלֹהֵינוּ	Baruch atah יהוה Eloheinu
מֶלֶךְ הָעוֹלָם, הָאֵל הָאָב הָרַחֲמָן,	melech ha·olam, ha-El ha·av harachaman
הַמְהֻלָּל בְּפִי עַמּוֹ, מְשֻׁבָּח וּמְפֹאָר	ham'hulal b'fi amo m'shubach um'fo·ar
בִּלְשׁוֹן חֲסִידָיו וַעֲבָדָיו,	bil'shon chasidav va·avodav
וּבְשִׁירֵי דָוִד עַבְדֶּךָ.	uv'shirei David avdecha.
נְהַלֶּלְךָ יהוה אֱלֹהֵינוּ בִּשְׁבָחוֹת	N'halel'cha יהוה Eloheinu bishvachot
וּבִזְמִרוֹת, נְגַדֶּלְךָ וּנְשַׁבֵּחֲךָ	uvizmirot n'gadelcha un'sh'beichacha
וּנְפָאֶרְךָ וְנַזְכִּיר שִׁמְךָ, וְנַמְלִיכְךָ,	u'nfa·ercha v'nazkir shimcha v'namlich'cha
מַלְכֵּנוּ אֱלֹהֵינוּ, יָחִיד, חֵי הָעוֹלָמִים,	malkeinu Eloheinu yachid chei ha·olamim
מֶלֶךְ מְשֻׁבָּח וּמְפֹאָר עֲדֵי עַד	melech m'shubach um'fo·ar adei ad
שְׁמוֹ הַגָּדוֹל.	sh'mo hagadol.
בָּרוּךְ אַתָּה יהוה,	Baruch atah יהוה
מֶלֶךְ מְהֻלָּל בַּתִּשְׁבָּחוֹת.	melech m'hulal b'tishbachot.

Blessed are You, יהוה our God, Source of all that is, Source of mercy, whose praises are sung in every mouth. With the songs of David, Your servant, we will praise You, יהוה our God. You alone are the life of the universe. You are our Eternal Source.
Blessed are You, יהוה our God, praised in song.

From Psalm 30

אֵלֶיךָ יהוה אֶקְרָא, Eleicha יהוה ekra,
וְאֶל אֲדֹנָי אֶתְחַנָּן. v'el יהוה etchanan.
שְׁמַע יהוה וְחָנֵּנִי, Sh'ma, יהוה, v'choneini
יהוה הֱיֵה עֹזֵר לִי. יהוה heyeh ozer li.

Answer me, God, when I cry.
Hear me and be merciful; You are my help!

Mourner's Kaddish

יִתְגַּדַּל וְיִתְקַדַּשׁ שְׁמֵהּ רַבָּא. Yitgadal v'yitkadash, sh'meih raba. (Amen)
בְּעָלְמָא דִּי בְרָא כִרְעוּתֵהּ, b'alma di v'ra chiruteih,
וְיַמְלִיךְ מַלְכוּתֵהּ V'yamlich malchuteih

In communities that follow nusach sefarad:

(וְיַצְמַח פֻּרְקָנֵהּ וִיקָרֵב מְשִׁיחֵהּ) (v'yakreiv m'shicheih v'yatzmach purkaneih)

בְּחַיֵּיכוֹן וּבְיוֹמֵיכוֹן b'chayeichon uvyomeichon,
וּבְחַיֵּי דְכָל בֵּית יִשְׂרָאֵל. uvchayei d'chol beit Yisra·el.
בַּעֲגָלָא וּבִזְמַן קָרִיב וְאִמְרוּ אָמֵן. ba·agala uvizman kariv; v'imru: **Amen.**

**יְהֵא שְׁמֵהּ רַבָּא מְבָרַךְ Y'hei sh'meih raba m'varach
לְעָלַם וּלְעָלְמֵי עָלְמַיָּא. l'alam ul·almei almaya.**

יִתְבָּרַךְ וְיִשְׁתַּבַּח, וְיִתְפָּאַר Yitbarach v'yishtabach, v'yitpa·ar
וְיִתְרוֹמַם וְיִתְנַשֵּׂא וְיִתְהַדָּר v'yit·romam v'yitnasei v'yit·hadar
וְיִתְעַלֶּה וְיִתְהַלָּל שְׁמֵהּ דְּקֻדְשָׁא v'yitaleh v'yit·halal sh'meih d'kudsha
בְּרִיךְ הוּא - b'rich hu -
לְעֵלָּא l'eila

During the Ten Days of Repentance:
וּלְעֵלָּא uleila

מִן כָּל בִּרְכָתָא וְשִׁירָתָא,   min kol birchata v'shirata,
תֻּשְׁבְּחָתָא וְנֶחֱמָתָא, דַּאֲמִירָן   tushb'chata v'nechemata da·amiran
בְּעָלְמָא, וְאִמְרוּ **אָמֵן**.   b'alma; v'imru: **Amen.**

יְהֵא שְׁלָמָא רַבָּא מִן שְׁמַיָּא   Y'hei sh'lama raba min sh'maya
וְחַיִּים עָלֵינוּ וְעַל כָּל יִשְׂרָאֵל,   v'chayim aleinu v'al kol Yisra·el;
וְאִמְרוּ **אָמֵן**.   v'imru: **Amen.**

עֹשֶׂה שָׁלוֹם בִּמְרוֹמָיו   Oseh shalom bimromav,
הוּא יַעֲשֶׂה שָׁלוֹם   hu ya·aseh shalom
עָלֵינוּ וְעַל כָּל יִשְׂרָאֵל,   aleinu, v'al kol Yisra·el,
וְעַל כָּל יוֹשְׁבֵי תֵבֵל, וְאִמְרוּ **אָמֵן**.   v'al kol yoshvei teiveil; v'imru: **Amen.**

I pray to You God,
that the power residing in Your Great Name
be increased and made sacred
in this world which God created freely
in order to preside in it, and grow its freeing power
and bring about the messianic era.
May this happen during our lifetime
and during the lifetime of all of us
living now, the house of Israel.
May this happen soon, without delay
and by saying AMEN we express agreement and hope, **AMEN**.

May that immense power residing in God's great name
flow freely into our world and worlds beyond.

May that Great Name, that sacred energy,
be shaped
and made effective
and be acknowledged
and be given the right honor
and be seen as beautiful
and uplifting
and bring jubilation.
Way beyond our input
of worshipful song and praise
which we express in this world
as our agreement and hope, **AMEN**.

May that endless peace
that heaven can release for us
bring about the good life
for us and for all Israel
as we express our agreement and hope, **AMEN.**

You, who harmonize it all
on the highest planes:
bring harmony and peace to us,
to all Israel and all sentient beings
as we express our agreement and hope, **AMEN.**

(translation: R' Zalman Schachter-Shalomi z"l)

from Psalm 92

מִזְמוֹר שִׁיר לְיוֹם הַשַּׁבָּת. Mizmor shir l'yom haShabbat:

טוֹב לְהֹדוֹת לַיהוה Tov l'hodot la-יהוה
וּלְזַמֵּר לְשִׁמְךָ עֶלְיוֹן. ul'zamer l'shimcha elyon.

לְהַגִּיד בַּבֹּקֶר חַסְדֶּךָ L'hagid baboker chasdecha,
וֶאֱמוּנָתְךָ בַּלֵּילוֹת. v'emunatecha baleilot.

עֲלֵי עָשׂוֹר וַעֲלֵי נָבֶל Alei asor va·alei navel
עֲלֵי הִגָּיוֹן בְּכִנּוֹר. alei higayon b'chinor.

A psalm. A song of the day Shabbat.

How good it is to praise Adonai
and to sing to God on high:

To tell of Your love in the morning
and of your faithfulness at night!

I sing to the music of the harp,
to the sound of string and voice.

כִּי שִׂמַּחְתַּנִי יהוה בְּפָעֳלֶךָ Ki samachtani יהוה b'fo·alecha
בְּמַעֲשֵׂי יָדֶיךָ אֲרַנֵּן. B'ma·asei yadecha aranen.

מַה גָּדְלוּ מַעֲשֶׂיךָ יהוה Mah gadlu ma·asecha יהוה
מְאֹד עָמְקוּ מַחְשְׁבֹתֶיךָ. Me·od amku mach'sh'votecha.

For You have made me rejoice, יהוה.
I thrill at the beauty of Your world.

How great is Your work, יהוה:
How profound is the world's design!

Ashrei

Short Ashrei Chant

אַשְׁרֵי יוֹשְׁבֵי בֵיתֶךָ, עוֹד יְהַלְלוּךָ סֶּלָה.

Ashrei yosh'vei veitecha. Od y'hal'lucha selah.

Happy are they who dwell in Your house; they will praise You forever.

Full-Text Ashrei

אַשְׁרֵי יוֹשְׁבֵי בֵיתֶךָ, Ashrei yosh'vei veitecha
עוֹד יְהַלְלוּךָ סֶּלָה. od y'hal'lucha selah.
אַשְׁרֵי הָעָם שֶׁכָּכָה לּוֹ, Ashrei ha·am shekacha lo,
אַשְׁרֵי הָעָם שֶׁיהוה אֱלֹהָיו. Ashrei ha·am sh'יהוה Elohav.

תְּהִלָּה לְדָוִד, T'hilah leDavid.

אֲרוֹמִמְךָ אֱלוֹהַי הַמֶּלֶךְ, Aromimcha Elohai hamelech
וַאֲבָרְכָה שִׁמְךָ לְעוֹלָם וָעֶד. va·avar'cha shimcha l'olam va·ed.
בְּכָל יוֹם אֲבָרְכֶךָּ, B'chol yom avar'cheka
וַאֲהַלְלָה שִׁמְךָ לְעוֹלָם וָעֶד. va·ahal'la shimcha l'olam va·ed.
גָּדוֹל יהוה וּמְהֻלָּל מְאֹד, Gadol יהוה umhulal m'od;
וְלִגְדֻלָּתוֹ אֵין חֵקֶר. v'ligdulato ein cheiker.
דּוֹר לְדוֹר יְשַׁבַּח מַעֲשֶׂיךָ, Dor ledor y'shabach ma·asecha
וּגְבוּרֹתֶיךָ יַגִּידוּ. ugvurotecha yagidu.

הֲדַר כְּבוֹד הוֹדֶךָ,	Hadar k'vod hodecha;
וְדִבְרֵי נִפְלְאֹתֶיךָ אָשִׂיחָה.	v'divrei nifl'otecha asichah.
וֶעֱזוּז נוֹרְאוֹתֶיךָ יֹאמֵרוּ,	Ve-ezuz nor'otecha yomeiru;
וּגְדֻלָּתְךָ אֲסַפְּרֶנָּה.	ugdulat'cha asap'renah.
זֵכֶר רַב טוּבְךָ יַבִּיעוּ,	Zeicher rav tuv'cha yabiu;
וְצִדְקָתְךָ יְרַנֵּנוּ.	v'tzidkat'cha y'raneinu.
חַנּוּן וְרַחוּם יהוה,	Chanun v'rachum יהוה;
אֶרֶךְ אַפַּיִם וּגְדָל חָסֶד.	erech apayim ugdol chased.
טוֹב יהוה לַכֹּל,	Tov יהוה lakol;
וְרַחֲמָיו עַל כָּל מַעֲשָׂיו.	v'rachamav al kol ma·asav.
יוֹדוּךָ יהוה כָּל מַעֲשֶׂיךָ,	Yoducha יהוה kolma·asecha;
וַחֲסִידֶיךָ יְבָרְכוּכָה.	vachasidecha y'varchucha.
כְּבוֹד מַלְכוּתְךָ יֹאמֵרוּ,	K'vod malchut'cha yomeiru;
וּגְבוּרָתְךָ יְדַבֵּרוּ.	ugvurat'cha y'dabeiru.
לְהוֹדִיעַ לִבְנֵי הָאָדָם גְּבוּרֹתָיו,	L'hodia livnei ha·adam g'vurotav,
וּכְבוֹד הֲדַר מַלְכוּתוֹ.	uchvod hadar malchuto.
מַלְכוּתְךָ מַלְכוּת כָּל עוֹלָמִים,	Malchut'cha malchut kol olamim,
וּמֶמְשַׁלְתְּךָ בְּכָל דֹּר וָדֹר.	umemshalt'cha b'choldor vador.
סוֹמֵךְ יהוה לְכָל הַנֹּפְלִים,	Someich יהוה l'chol hanof'lim,
וְזוֹקֵף לְכָל הַכְּפוּפִים.	v'zokef l'chol hak'fufim.
עֵינֵי כֹל אֵלֶיךָ יְשַׂבֵּרוּ,	Einei chol eilecha y'sabeiru;
וְאַתָּה נוֹתֵן לָהֶם אֶת אָכְלָם בְּעִתּוֹ.	v'atah notein lahem et-ochlam b'ito.
פּוֹתֵחַ אֶת יָדֶךָ,	Potei·ach et yadecha,
וּמַשְׂבִּיעַ לְכָל חַי רָצוֹן.	umasbia l'chol-chai ratzon.
צַדִּיק יהוה בְּכָל דְּרָכָיו,	Tzaddik יהוה b'chol d'rachav,
וְחָסִיד בְּכָל מַעֲשָׂיו.	v'chasid b'chol ma·asav.
קָרוֹב יהוה לְכָל קֹרְאָיו,	Karov יהוה l'chol kor'av,
לְכֹל אֲשֶׁר יִקְרָאֻהוּ בֶאֱמֶת.	l'chol asher yikra·uhu ve-emet.
רְצוֹן יְרֵאָיו יַעֲשֶׂה,	R'tzon y'rei·av ya·aseh;
וְאֶת שַׁוְעָתָם יִשְׁמַע וְיוֹשִׁיעֵם.	v'et shavatam yish'ma v'yoshi·eim.
שׁוֹמֵר יהוה אֶת כָּל אֹהֲבָיו,	Shomeir יהוה et kol ohavav;
וְאֵת כָּל הָרְשָׁעִים יַשְׁמִיד.	v'et kol har'sha·im yashmid.
תְּהִלַּת יהוה יְדַבֶּר פִּי,	T'hilat יהוה y'daber pi;
וִיבָרֵךְ כָּל בָּשָׂר	vivareich kol basar
שֵׁם קָדְשׁוֹ לְעוֹלָם וָעֶד.	shem kodsho l'olam va·ed.
וַאֲנַחְנוּ נְבָרֵךְ יָהּ,	Va·anachnu n'vareich Yah
מֵעַתָּה וְעַד עוֹלָם, הַלְלוּיָהּ.	me-atah v'ad olam, hal'lu-Yah!

Full-Text Ashrei

Happy are they who dwell in Your house; may they continue to praise You!
Happy is the people for whom life is thus;
happy is the people with the Everlasting for its God!

A Psalm of David:

All exaltations I raise to You; I bless Your name forever.
Blessings do I offer You each day; I hail Your name, forever!
Great is the Eternal, to be praised; God's greatness is boundless.
Declaring praises for Your deeds, we describe Your mighty acts.
Heaven's splendor is my song; words of Your miracles I sing.
Wondrous are Your powers; we tell of Your magnificence.
Signs of Your abundant goodness we express; in Your justice we rejoice.
Gracious and merciful are You; slow to anger, great in love.
To all God's creatures, goodness flows; on all creation, love.
Your creatures all give thanks to You and bless You.
Calling out Your sovereign glory, we speak Your magnificence.
Letting all know Your mighty acts, Your glory and splendor.
May Your sovereignty last all eternities, Your dominion forever.
Strong support to all who fall, God raises up the humble & lame.
All gazes turn toward You for sustenance in its appointed time.
Providing with Your open hand, You satisfy desire in all life.
So just is God in every way, so loving amid all the divine deeds.
Close by is God to all who call, to all who call to God in truth.
Responding to yearning and awe, God hears their cry & rescues.
Showing care to all who love God, God destroys evildoing.
The praise of God my mouth declares; all flesh blesses the Holy Name forever.
And as for us, we bless the name of Yah, from now until the end of time.
Halleluyah!

Renewed Ashrei

This variation on the Ashrei uses quotations from His Holiness the Dalai Lama to articulate the themes of the Ashrei. Like the classical Ashrei, it is an alphabetical acrostic.

If you want others to be happy, practice compassion.
If you want to be happy, practice compassion.

Account for the fact that great love / and great achievements involve great risk.
But when you lose at something you attempted / don't lose the lesson.
Chart by the three R's: / Respect for self, Respect for others and Responsibility.
Don't forget that not getting what you want / is sometimes a stroke of luck.
Each time you realize you've made a mistake / take immediate steps to correct it.
Friendships include differences / don't let a dispute injure a relationship.
Genuine friends will stand by you / whether you are successful or unlucky.
Happiness is not something ready made. / It comes from your own actions.
In disagreements deal only with the current situation. / Don't bring up the past.
Judge success by what you gave up / in order to get what you wanted.
Keep an open heart / everyone needs to be loved.
Love and compassion are necessities. / Without them, humanity cannot survive.
Maintain a sincere attitude / be concerned that outcomes are fair
Nurture a loving atmosphere in your home / it is the foundation for your life.
Open your arms to change / but don't let go of your values.
Please be gentle with the earth / it's the only planet we have.
Quit complaining about others / and spend more time making yourself better.
Remember that silence … / … is sometimes the best answer.
Share your knowledge wisely. / It is a way to achieve immortality.
Twice or even once a year / go someplace you've never been before.
Understanding for others / brings the tranquility and happiness we seek.
Verify your understanding / but don't forget to believe and have faith.
We all need some time alone / make room for you each and every day.
X-ray vision doesn't exist / but seeking the truth is a good start.
You are not alone / God made all of us unique but not special.
Zero in on what matters / and start each day with loving yourself.

(Rabbi Evan Krame)

Psalm 136 / Ki L'Olam Chasdo

הוֹדוּ לַיהוה כִּי טוֹב, כִּי לְעוֹלָם חַסְדּוֹ	Hodu la-יהוה ki tov: ki l'olam chasdo.
הוֹדוּ לֵאלֹהֵי הָאֱלֹהִים, כִּי לְעוֹלָם חַסְדּוֹ	Hodu le-Elohei ha-elohim...
הוֹדוּ לַאֲדֹנֵי הָאֲדֹנִים, כִּי לְעוֹלָם חַסְדּוֹ	Hodu la-Adonei ha-adonim...
לְעֹשֵׂה נִפְלָאוֹת גְּדֹלוֹת לְבַדּוֹ, כִּי לְעוֹלָם חַסְדּוֹ	Le·oseh nifla·ot gedolot levado...
לְעֹשֵׂה הַשָּׁמַיִם בִּתְבוּנָה, כִּי לְעוֹלָם חַסְדּוֹ	Le·oseh shamayim bitvunah...
לְרוֹקַע הָאָרֶץ עַל הַמָּיִם, כִּי לְעוֹלָם חַסְדּוֹ	Leroka ha·ara·etz al hamayim...
לְעֹשֵׂה אוֹרִים גְּדֹלִים, כִּי לְעוֹלָם חַסְדּוֹ	Le·oseh orim gedolim...
אֶת הַשֶּׁמֶשׁ לְמֶמְשֶׁלֶת בַּיּוֹם, כִּי לְעוֹלָם חַסְדּוֹ	Et hashemesh lememshelet bayom...
אֶת הַיָּרֵחַ וְכוֹכָבִים לְמֶמְשְׁלוֹת בַּלָּיְלָה, כִּי לְעוֹלָם חַסְדּוֹ	Et yare·ach vechochavim lememsh'lot balayla...
לְמַכֵּה מִצְרַיִם בִּבְכוֹרֵיהֶם, כִּי לְעוֹלָם חַסְדּוֹ	L'makeh Mitzrayim bivchoreihem...
וַיּוֹצֵא יִשְׂרָאֵל מִתּוֹכָם, כִּי לְעוֹלָם חַסְדּוֹ	Veyotzei Yisra·el mitocham...
בְּיָד חֲזָקָה וּבִזְרוֹעַ נְטוּיָה, כִּי לְעוֹלָם חַסְדּוֹ	Beyad chazakah uvizro·a netuyah...
לְגֹזֵר יַם סוּף לִגְזָרִים, כִּי לְעוֹלָם חַסְדּוֹ	L'gozer yam suf ligzarim...
וְהֶעֱבִיר יִשְׂרָאֵל בְּתוֹכוֹ, כִּי לְעוֹלָם חַסְדּוֹ	V'he·evir Yisra·el betocho...
וְנִעֵר פַּרְעֹה וְחֵילוֹ בְיַם סוּף, כִּי לְעוֹלָם חַסְדּוֹ	V'ni·er Paro v'cheilo beyam suf...
לְמוֹלִיךְ עַמּוֹ בַּמִּדְבָּר, כִּי לְעוֹלָם חַסְדּוֹ	L'molich amo bamidbar...
לְמַכֵּה מְלָכִים גְּדֹלִים, כִּי לְעוֹלָם חַסְדּוֹ	L'makeh m'lachim g'dolim...
וַיַּהֲרֹג מְלָכִים אַדִּירִים, כִּי לְעוֹלָם חַסְדּוֹ	Vayaharog m'lachim adirim...
לְסִיחוֹן מֶלֶךְ הָאֱמֹרִי, כִּי לְעוֹלָם חַסְדּוֹ	L'Sichon melech ha·emori...
וּלְעוֹג מֶלֶךְ הַבָּשָׁן, כִּי לְעוֹלָם חַסְדּוֹ	Ul'Og melech habashan...
וְנָתַן אַרְצָם לְנַחֲלָה, כִּי לְעוֹלָם חַסְדּוֹ	V'natan artzam l'nachalah...
נַחֲלָה לְיִשְׂרָאֵל עַבְדּוֹ, כִּי לְעוֹלָם חַסְדּוֹ	Nachala leYisra·el avdo...
שֶׁבְּשִׁפְלֵנוּ זָכַר לָנוּ, כִּי לְעוֹלָם חַסְדּוֹ	Sheb'shifleinu zachar lanu...
וַיִּפְרְקֵנוּ מִצָּרֵינוּ, כִּי לְעוֹלָם חַסְדּוֹ	Vayif're'keinu mitzareinu...
נֹתֵן לֶחֶם לְכָל בָּשָׂר, כִּי לְעוֹלָם חַסְדּוֹ	Notein lechem lechol basar...
הוֹדוּ לְאֵל הַשָּׁמַיִם, כִּי לְעוֹלָם חַסְדּוֹ	Hodu le·El hashamayim ki l'olam chasdo!

Praise יהוה for God is good, God's steadfast love is eternal.
Praise the God of gods, God's steadfast love is eternal.
Praise the Lord of lords, God's steadfast love is eternal;
Who alone works great marvels, God's steadfast love is eternal;
Who made the heavens with wisdom, God's steadfast love is eternal;
Who spread the earth over the water, God's steadfast love is eternal;
Who made the great lights, God's steadfast love is eternal;
the sun to dominate the day, God's steadfast love is eternal;
the moon and the stars to dominate the night, God's steadfast love is eternal;
Who struck Egypt through their first-born, God's steadfast love is eternal;
and brought Israel out of their midst, God's steadfast love is eternal;
with a strong hand and outstretched arm, God's steadfast love is eternal;
Who split apart the Sea of Reeds, God's steadfast love is eternal;
and made Israel pass through it, God's steadfast love is eternal;
Who hurled Pharaoh and his army into the Sea of Reeds,
God's steadfast love is eternal;
Who led His people through the wilderness, God's steadfast love is eternal;
Who struck down great kings, God's steadfast love is eternal;
and slew mighty kings— God's steadfast love is eternal;
Sihon, king of the Amorites, God's steadfast love is eternal;
Og, king of Bashan— God's steadfast love is eternal;
and gave their land as a heritage, God's steadfast love is eternal;
a heritage to God's servant Israel, God's steadfast love is eternal;
Who took note of us in our degradation, God's steadfast love is eternal;
and rescued us from our enemies, God's steadfast love is eternal;
Who gives food to all flesh, God's steadfast love is eternal.
Praise the God of heaven, God's steadfast love is eternal.

Body Hodu (Psalm 136)

הוֹדוּ לַיהוה כִּי טוֹב,   Hodu La-יהוה ki tov
כִּי לְעוֹלָם חַסְדּוֹ.   Ki l'olam chasdo

    Praise יהוה for God is good,
    God's steadfast love is eternal.

Thanks and praises for all your blessings
Ki l'olam chasdo / כִּי לְעוֹלָם חַסְדּוֹ
For our toes and feet that ground us …
For our legs and hips that move us …
For our organs that bring us pleasure …
For our bellies that transform nourishment …
For our lungs that breathe your spirit …
For our hearts that can feel your love …
For our arms and hands for creating …
For our throats that birth our voices …
For our mouths that speak your truth …
For our tongues that taste your bounty …
For our noses that smell your fragrances …
For our ears that hear your music …
For our eyes that see your beauty …
For our minds that comprehend your holiness …
For our souls you have planted within us. …

הוֹדוּ לְאֵל הַשָּׁמַיִם,   Hodu le-El hashamayim
כִּי לְעוֹלָם חַסְדּוֹ.   ki l'olam chasdo!

    Praise to the God of heaven,
    God's steadfast love is eternal!

(Rabba Kaya Stern-Kaufman)

Psalm 148

הַלְלוּיָהּ, הַלְלוּ אֶת יהוה מִן הַשָּׁמַיִם
הַלְלוּהוּ בַּמְּרוֹמִים. הַלְלוּהוּ כָל מַלְאָכָיו,
הַלְלוּהוּ כָּל צְבָאָיו.
הַלְלוּהוּ שֶׁמֶשׁ וְיָרֵחַ, הַלְלוּהוּ כָּל
כּוֹכְבֵי אוֹר. הַלְלוּהוּ שְׁמֵי הַשָּׁמָיִם,
וְהַמַּיִם אֲשֶׁר מֵעַל הַשָּׁמָיִם.
יְהַלְלוּ אֶת שֵׁם יהוה
כִּי הוּא צִוָּה וְנִבְרָאוּ. וַיַּעֲמִידֵם לָעַד
לְעוֹלָם, חָק נָתַן וְלֹא יַעֲבוֹר.
הַלְלוּ אֶת יהוה מִן הָאָרֶץ, תַּנִּינִים
וְכָל תְּהֹמוֹת. אֵשׁ וּבָרָד שֶׁלֶג וְקִיטוֹר,
רוּחַ סְעָרָה עֹשָׂה דְבָרוֹ. הֶהָרִים וְכָל
גְּבָעוֹת, עֵץ פְּרִי וְכָל אֲרָזִים. הַחַיָּה
וְכָל בְּהֵמָה, רֶמֶשׂ וְצִפּוֹר כָּנָף.
מַלְכֵי אֶרֶץ וְכָל לְאֻמִּים
שָׂרִים וְכָל שֹׁפְטֵי אָרֶץ. בַּחוּרִים
וְגַם בְּתוּלוֹת, זְקֵנִים עִם נְעָרִים.
יְהַלְלוּ אֶת שֵׁם יהוה, כִּי נִשְׂגָּב שְׁמוֹ לְבַדּוֹ
הוֹדוֹ עַל אֶרֶץ וְשָׁמָיִם.
וַיָּרֶם קֶרֶן לְעַמּוֹ תְּהִלָּה לְכָל חֲסִידָיו
לִבְנֵי יִשְׂרָאֵל עַם קְרֹבוֹ הַלְלוּיָהּ.

Hal'lu·Yah, hallelu et יהוה min hashamayim, haleluhu ba-m'romim. Halleluhu kol melachav, halleluhu kol tzeva·av. Halleluhu shemesh v'yare·ach, halleluhu kol kochvei or. Halleluhu shmei hashamayim, v'hamyim asher m'al hashamayim. Y'hallelu et shem יהוה ki hu tziva v'niv'ra·u. Vaya·amidem la·ad l'olam, chok natan v'lo ya·avor. Hallelu et יהוה min ha·aretz taninim v'chol t'homot. Esh uvarad sheleg v'kitor, ruach s'arah osah d'varo. Heharim v'chol givaot, etz pri v'chol arazim. Hachayah v'chol b'hemah, remes v'tzipor kanaf. Malchei eretz v'chol l'umim sarim v'chol shoftei aretz. Bachurim v'gam b'tulot, z'kenim im n'arim. Y'hallelu et shem יהוה ki nisgav shemo l'vado. Hodo al eretz v'shamayim. Vayarem keren l'amo t'hilah l'chol chasidav liv'nei Yisra·el am k'rovo hal'lu·Yah.

Hallelujah. Praise יהוה from the heavens; praise God on high.
Praise God, all angels, praise God, all heavenly hosts.
Praise God, sun and moon, praise God, all bright stars.
Praise God, highest heavens, and you waters that are above the heavens.
Let them praise the name of יהוה,
for it was God who commanded that they be created.
God made them endure forever, establishing an order that shall never change.
Praise יהוה, O you who are on earth, all sea monsters and ocean depths,
fire and hail, snow and smoke, storm wind that executes His command,
all mountains and hills, all fruit trees and cedars,
all wild and tamed beasts, creeping things and winged birds,
all kings and peoples of the earth, all princes of the earth and its judges,
youths and maidens alike, old and young together.
Let them praise the name of יהוה, for God's name, God's alone, is sublime; God's
splendor covers heaven and earth.
God has exalted the horn of God's people for the glory of all God's faithful ones,
Israel, the people close to God. Hallelujah.

Psalm 150

הַלְלוּיָהּ!	Hal'lu·Yah!
הַלְלוּ אֵל בְּקָדְשׁוֹ, הַלְלוּהוּ בִּרְקִיעַ עֻזּוֹ.	Halelu El bekodsho, haleluhu birkia uzo.
הַלְלוּהוּ בִגְבוּרֹתָיו, הַלְלוּהוּ כְּרֹב גֻּדְלוֹ.	Haleluhu bigvurotav, haleluhu k'rov gudlo.
הַלְלוּהוּ בְּתֵקַע שׁוֹפָר,	Haleluhu b'teika shofar,
הַלְלוּהוּ בְּנֵבֶל וְכִנּוֹר.	haleluhu b'neivel vechinor.
הַלְלוּהוּ בְּתֹף וּמָחוֹל,	Haleluhu b'tof umachol,
הַלְלוּהוּ בְּמִנִּים וְעֻגָב.	haleluhu b'minim ve·ugav.
הַלְלוּהוּ בְצִלְצְלֵי שָׁמַע,	Haleluhu b'tziltz'lei shama,
הַלְלוּהוּ בְּצִלְצְלֵי תְרוּעָה.	haleluhu b'tziltz'lei t'ru·ah.
כֹּל הַנְּשָׁמָה תְּהַלֵּל יָהּ הַלְלוּיָהּ.	Kol han'shamah tehallel Yah, hal'lu·Yah.

Hallelujah.
Praise God in holy places, praise God in the sky.
Praise God for might, praise God for greatness.
Praise God with shofar blasts, praise God with harp and lyre.
Praise God with song and dance, praise God with lute and pipe.
Praise God with cymbals, praise God with their crash.
Let all that breathes praise God. Hallelujah.

Give Praise

Give praise for every breath you take
Give praise every time you open your eyes
Give praise when you're reading or speaking
Give praise for every mitzvah or every sin
Give praise for all that you feel
Give praise because you're alive and you can
Give praise whether you want to or not

(Rachael Hermann)

From *Nishmat Kol Chai:* The Breath of All Life

נִשְׁמַת כָּל חַי   Nishmat kol chai
תְּבָרֵךְ אֶת שִׁמְךָ יהוה אֱלֹהֵינוּ.   t'varech et shimcha יהוה Eloheinu.
וְרוּחַ כָּל בָּשָׂר, תְּפָאֵר וּתְרוֹמֵם   V'ruach kol basar, t'fa·er ut·romem
זִכְרְךָ מַלְכֵּנוּ תָּמִיד,   zichrecha malkeinu tamid,
מִן הָעוֹלָם וְעַד הָעוֹלָם אַתָּה אֵל.   min ha·olam v'ad ha·olam atah El.

The breath of all life will bless Your name, יהוה
our God, the spirit of our bodies.
We praise and exalt You,
from one reality to the next:
You are God.

אִלּוּ פִינוּ מָלֵא שִׁירָה כַּיָּם...   Ilu finu maleh shirah kayam...

Were our mouths filled with song as the sea
our tongues joyful like the waves
our lips filled with praise as the heavens
our eyes brilliant like the sun and the moon
our hands outspread as eagle's wings
our feet as swift as deers',
it would not be enough to thank You,
our God of eternity and eternities.

Nishmat

Souls are silent
But breath is a prayer
Rolling slowly
Bearer of life's gift
In and out.

All breath prays
A fleeing mouse
A diving owl
A flower celebrating the sun
A wind pushing through between my legs.

Lovers between kisses
Young folks working
Old folks resting
Children being
Always praying
Always blessing
Always praising

The breath of all life praises your name, Dear God.

(Rabbi Lewis John Eron)

PSUKEI D'ZIMRA: PSALMS OF PRAISE

בָּרְכִי נַפְשִׁי אֶת יהוה,   Barchi nafshi et יהוה,
וְכָל קְרָבַי אֶת שֵׁם קָדְשׁוֹ.   v'chol kravai et shem kodsho.
הָאֵל בְּתַעֲצֻמוֹת עֻזֶּךָ,   Ha·El b'ta·atzumot uzecha,
הַגָּדוֹל בִּכְבוֹד שְׁמֶךָ.   Hagadol bichvod sh'mecha.
הַגִּבּוֹר לָנֶצַח וְהַנּוֹרָא בְּנוֹרְאוֹתֶיךָ.   Hagibor lanetzach v'hanora b'norotecha.
הַמֶּלֶךְ הַיּוֹשֵׁב עַל כִּסֵּא רָם וְנִשָּׂא.   Hamelech hayosheiv al kisei ram v'nisa.

Bless יהוה, O my soul!
And let all that is within me praise the holy Name.
O God, in the power of Your strength,
Great in the glory of Your Name,
Mighty forever, Awesome in amazing deeds,
Majestic One who presides over all destiny!

שׁוֹכֵן עַד מָרוֹם וְקָדוֹשׁ שְׁמוֹ.   Shochein ad marom v'kadosh sh'mo.
וְכָתוּב, רַנְּנוּ צַדִּיקִים בַּיהוה,   V'chatuv: ran'nu tzadikim b'יהוה,
לַיְשָׁרִים נָאוָה תְהִלָּה.   lay'sharim nava t'hilah.

בְּפִי יְשָׁרִים תִּתְרוֹמָם.   B'fi **y**'sharim tit·**r**omam,
וּבְדִבְרֵי צַדִּיקִים תִּתְבָּרַךְ.   uv'divrei **tz**adikim tit**b**arach,
וּבִלְשׁוֹן חֲסִידִים תִּתְקַדָּשׁ.   uvilshon **ch**asidim tit**k**adash,
וּבְקֶרֶב קְדוֹשִׁים תִּתְהַלָּל.   uv'kerev **k**'doshim tit'**h**alal.

Eternal Shekhinah, Holy Beyond:
Saints sing Your name
In harmony with the upright.

Good people exalt You
Saints are Your blessing
Devotees sanctify You
You delight in our inner holiness.

(translation: R' Zalman Schachter-Shalomi z"l)

    In the second stanza of the Hebrew above, the enlarged Hebrew letters highlight an acrostic which spells "Yitzchak" and "Rivkah," Isaac and Rebecca. If we add the numerical values (gematria) of those two Hebrew names, we get the numerical value of the word "tefilah," prayer. This teaches that our prayer reaches its highest form when our communities are inclusive of all genders.

Yishtabach: Blessing Ending *Psukei D'Zimrah*

יִשְׁתַּבַּח שִׁמְךָ לָעַד מַלְכֵּנוּ,
הָאֵל הַמֶּלֶךְ הַגָּדוֹל וְהַקָּדוֹשׁ
בַּשָּׁמַיִם וּבָאָרֶץ.
כִּי לְךָ נָאֶה יהוה אֱלֹהֵינוּ
וֵאלֹהֵי אֲבוֹתֵינוּ וְאִמּוֹתֵינוּ
שִׁיר וּשְׁבָחָה הַלֵּל וְזִמְרָה
עֹז וּמֶמְשָׁלָה נֶצַח גְּדֻלָּה וּגְבוּרָה
תְּהִלָּה וְתִפְאֶרֶת קְדֻשָּׁה וּמַלְכוּת
בְּרָכוֹת וְהוֹדָאוֹת מֵעַתָּה וְעַד עוֹלָם.

Yishtabach shimcha la·ad malkeinu,
ha·El hamelech hagadol v'hakadosh
bashamayim uva·aretz.
Ki lecha na·eh יהוה Eloheinu
v'Elohei avoteinu v'imoteinu
shir u'shvacha hallel v'zimrah
oz umemshalah netzach g'dulah ugvurah
t'hilah v'tiferet k'dushah umalchut
b'rachot v'hoda·ot m'atah v'ad olam.

בָּרוּךְ אַתָּה יהוה אֵל מֶלֶךְ גָּדוֹל
בַּתִּשְׁבָּחוֹת אֵל הַהוֹדָאוֹת
אֲדוֹן הַנִּפְלָאוֹת
הַבּוֹחֵר בְּשִׁירֵי זִמְרָה
מֶלֶךְ אֵל חֵי הָעוֹלָמִים.

Baruch atah יהוה El melech gadol
batishbachot El hahoda·ot
adon hanifla·ot
habocheir b'shirei zimrah
melech El chei ha·olamim.

May Your name be forever blessed, our source of being,
great and holy God, in heaven and on earth.
Songs and praise, adulation and melody,
strength and power, eternity, greatness and might,
blessing and thanks are the words we can use
to speak of יהוה, our God and God of our ancestors,
for now and evermore.

Blessed are You, יהוה, God who is greatly praised,
God who is thanked, master of miracles
who chooses songs of praise, the God of eternal life.

Your Name Be Praised

Your Name be praised, always
Majestic One,
Powerful and gentle Source,
Making Heaven and Earth sacred.

It is our pleasure to dedicate to You,
Our God and Our parents' God,
Time and again:

Music and Celebration,
Jubilation and Symphony,
Fortissimo, Anthem,
Victory March, Largo Forte,
Paean and Hymn,
Sanctus and Maestoso,
Laudo and Aria,
Celebrating Your Divine reputation
In every realm.

We worship You, Yah,
Generous, Great, Regal One
To whom we offer all these.

God whom we appreciate,
Source of all wonder,
Fountain of all souls,
Author of all that happens,
Who delights in music and chant
Origin of Unity.
You are the Life
That flows through all the worlds.
Amen.

(R' Zalman Schachter-Shalomi z"l)

The Kaddish: A Door

*In all of its forms, the Kaddish is a doorway
between one part of the service and the next.*

*As we move through this door, notice:
what is happening in your heart and mind?*

*Whatever is arising in you,
bring that into your prayer.*

Chatzi Kaddish

יִתְגַּדַּל וְיִתְקַדַּשׁ שְׁמֵהּ רַבָּא.
בְּעָלְמָא דִּי בְרָא כִרְעוּתֵהּ,
וְיַמְלִיךְ מַלְכוּתֵהּ.
בְּחַיֵּיכוֹן וּבְיוֹמֵיכוֹן, וּבְחַיֵּי דְכָל
בֵּית יִשְׂרָאֵל, בַּעֲגָלָא וּבִזְמַן קָרִיב
וְאִמְרוּ אָמֵן.

Yitgadal v'yitkadash sh'meih raba. (Amen)
b'alma di v'ra chiruteih,
v'yamlich malchuteih.
B'chayeichon uvyomeichon, uvchayei d'chol
beit Yisra·el, ba·agala uvizman kariv;
v'imru: **Amen.**

**יְהֵא שְׁמֵהּ רַבָּא מְבָרַךְ
לְעָלַם וּלְעָלְמֵי עָלְמַיָּא.**

**Y'hei sh'meih raba m'varakh
l'alam ul·almei almaya.**

יִתְבָּרַךְ וְיִשְׁתַּבַּח וְיִתְפָּאַר
וְיִתְרוֹמַם וְיִתְנַשֵּׂא וְיִתְהַדָּר
וְיִתְעַלֶּה וְיִתְהַלָּל שְׁמֵהּ דְּקֻדְשָׁא
בְּרִיךְ הוּא, לְעֵלָּא מִן כָּל בִּרְכָתָא
וְשִׁירָתָא תֻּשְׁבְּחָתָא וְנֶחֱמָתָא,
דַּאֲמִירָן בְּעָלְמָא, וְאִמְרוּ אָמֵן.

Yitbarach v'yishtabach v'yitpa·ar
v'yit·romam v'yitnasei v'yit·hadar
v'yitaleh v'yit'halal sh'meih d'kudsha
- **b'rich hu** - l'eila min kol birchata
v'shirata, tushb'chata v'nechemata,
da·amiran b'alma; v'imru: Amen.

Magnified and sanctified! Magnified and sanctified! May God's Great Name fill the world God created. May God's splendor be seen in the world in your life, in your days, in the life of all Israel. Quickly and soon! And let us say, Amen.
Forever may the Great Name be blessed!
Blessed and praised! Splendid and supreme! May the holy Name, Bless God, be praised, far beyond all the blessings and songs, comforts and consolations, that can be offered in this world. And let us say: Amen.

(Translated by Rabbi Daniel Brenner)

The Shema & Her Blessings

Bar'chu / Call to Prayer

Bar'chu, Dear One
Shechinah, Holy Name
As I call on the light of my soul, I come home.

(Lev Friedman)

בָּרְכוּ אֶת יהוה הַמְבֹרָךְ. Bar'chu et יהוה ham'vorach.
בָּרוּךְ יהוה הַמְבֹרָךְ לְעוֹלָם וָעֶד. Baruch יהוה ham'vorach l'olam va·ed.

Blessed is יהוה, the blessed One.
Blessed is יהוה, the blessed One, now and forever!

Yotzer Or / Blessing for Light

Yotzer Or Chant

בָּרוּךְ אַתָּה יהוה, Baruch atah יהוה,
אֱלֹהֵינוּ מֶלֶךְ הָעוֹלָם, Eloheinu melech ha-olam
יוֹצֵר אוֹר, וּבוֹרֵא חֹשֶׁךְ, Yotzer or uvorei choshech,
עֹשֶׂה שָׁלוֹם וּבוֹרֵא אֶת הַכֹּל. oseh shalom uvorei et hakol.

Blessed are You, יהוה, sovereign of all creation,
creator of light and former of darkness,
maker of peace and creator of all.

הַכֹּל יוֹדוּךָ, וְהַכֹּל יְשַׁבְּחוּךָ, Hakol yoducha, v'hakol y'shab'chucha
וְהַכֹּל יֹאמְרוּ אֵין קָדוֹשׁ כַּיהוה. V'hakol yomru ein kadosh ka-יהוה.

All that is will thank You; all that is will praise You;
and everything calls out, "None are holy like יהוה!"

אוֹר חָדָשׁ עַל צִיּוֹן תָּאִיר   Or chadash al tzion ta·ir
וְנִזְכֶּה כֻלָּנוּ מְהֵרָה לְאוֹרוֹ   V'nizkeh chulanu m'heirah l'oro.

May a new light shine upon Zion
and may we all swiftly merit its radiance.

Full text Yotzer Or

בָּרוּךְ אַתָּה יהוה,   Baruch atah יהוה
אֱלֹהֵינוּ מֶלֶךְ הָעוֹלָם,   Eloheinu melech ha·olam,
יוֹצֵר אוֹר, וּבוֹרֵא חֹשֶׁךְ,   yotzer or uvorei choshech,
עֹשֶׂה שָׁלוֹם וּבוֹרֵא אֶת הַכֹּל.   oseh shalom uvorei et hakol.

Blessed are You, יהוה our God, sovereign of all worlds:
creator of light and former of darkness,
maker of peace and creator of all things.

הַכֹּל יוֹדוּךָ, וְהַכֹּל יְשַׁבְּחוּךָ,   Hakol yoducha, v'hakol y'shab'chucha
וְהַכֹּל יֹאמְרוּ אֵין קָדוֹשׁ כַּיהוה.   V'hakol yomru ein kadosh ka-יהוה!

All that is will thank You; all that is will praise You;
and everything calls out, "None are holy like יהוה!"

הַכֹּל יְרוֹמְמוּךָ סֶּלָה, יוֹצֵר הַכֹּל.	Hakol y'rom'mukha selah, yotzer hakol.
הָאֵל הַפּוֹתֵחַ בְּכָל יוֹם	Ha·El hapoteich b'khol yom
דַּלְתוֹת שַׁעֲרֵי מִזְרָח,	daltot sha·arei mizrach,
וּבוֹקֵעַ חַלּוֹנֵי רָקִיעַ	uvokei·a chalonei raki·a
מוֹצִיא חַמָּה מִמְּקוֹמָהּ,	motzi chama mim'komah,
וּלְבָנָה מִמְּכוֹן שִׁבְתָּהּ,	ulvana mimkhon shiv'tah,
וּמֵאִיר לָעוֹלָם כֻּלּוֹ וּלְיוֹשְׁבָיו,	umei·ir la·olam kulo ul'yoshvav,
שֶׁבָּרָא בְּמִדַּת הָרַחֲמִים.	she'bara b'midat harachamim.
הַמֵּאִיר לָאָרֶץ	Hamei·ir la·aretz
וְלַדָּרִים עָלֶיהָ בְּרַחֲמִים.	v'ladarim aleha b'rachamim.
וּבְטוּבוֹ מְחַדֵּשׁ בְּכָל יוֹם תָּמִיד	Uv'tuvo m'chadeish b'khol yom tamid
מַעֲשֵׂה בְרֵאשִׁית.	ma·asei v'reishit.
הַמֶּלֶךְ הַמְרוֹמָם לְבַדּוֹ מֵאָז.	Hamelech ham'romam l'vado mei·az.
הַמְשֻׁבָּח וְהַמְפֹאָר וְהַמִּתְנַשֵּׂא	Ham'shubach v'ham'fo·ar v'hamitnasei
מִימוֹת עוֹלָם.	mimot olam.
אֱלֹהֵי עוֹלָם,	Elohei olam,
בְּרַחֲמֶיךָ הָרַבִּים רַחֵם עָלֵינוּ.	b'rachamekha harabim rachem aleinu.
אֲדוֹן עֻזֵּנוּ צוּר מִשְׂגַּבֵּנוּ,	Adon uzeinu tzur misgabeinu,
מָגֵן יִשְׁעֵנוּ, מִשְׂגָּב בַּעֲדֵנוּ. אֵין	magein y'sh·einu, misgav ba·adeinu.
כְּעֶרְכֶּךָ וְאֵין זוּלָתֶךָ, אֶפֶס בִּלְתֶּךָ,	Ein k'erke·kha v'ein zulatekha, efes bil'tekha,
וּמִי דּוֹמֶה לָךְ.	u'mi domeh lakh.
אֵין כְּעֶרְכְּךָ יְיָ אֱלֹהֵינוּ,	Ein k'erk'kha Adonai Eloheinu,
בָּעוֹלָם הַזֶּה, וְאֵין זוּלָתְךָ מַלְכֵּנוּ	ba·olam hazeh, v'ein zulat'kha malkeinu
לְחַיֵּי הָעוֹלָם הַבָּא.	l'chayei ha·olam haba.
אֶפֶס בִּלְתְּךָ גּוֹאֲלֵנוּ	Efes bilt'kha go·aleinu
לִימוֹת הַמָּשִׁיחַ. וְאֵין דּוֹמֶה לְךָ	limot hamashi·ach. V'ein domeh l'kha
מוֹשִׁיעֵנוּ לִתְחִיַּת הַמֵּתִים.	moshi·einu litchiyat hameitim.

All will exalt You forever, Creator of all. The All-mighty Who opens each day the doors of the gates of the east and pierces the windows of the firmament; Who brings the sun out of its place and the moon from its dwellingplace, and illumines the entire world and its inhabitants, whom God created with mercy.
God illuminates the earth and those who dwell upon it with compassion, and in God's goodness continually renews every day the work of creation.
The Sovereign Who alone is exalted, Who is praised, glorified, and uplifted from the beginning of time.
Eternal God, in Your abundant mercy, have compassion on us! God Who is our strength, Rock Who is our stronghold, Shield of our deliverance, be a stronghold for us. There is none to be compared to You, יהוה our God, in this world; and there is none beside You in the world to come. Nothing exists without You, Redeemer, and there will be none like You, Deliverer, even were the dead to return to life.

Yotzer Or / Blessing for Light

בָּרוּךְ אַתָּה יהוה,   Baruch atah יהוה
אֱלֹהֵינוּ מֶלֶךְ הָעוֹלָם,   Eloheinu melech ha·olam
יוֹצֵר אוֹר וּבוֹרֵא חֹשֶׁךְ,   Yotzer or uvorei choshech,
עֹשֶׂה שָׁלוֹם וּבוֹרֵא אֶת הַכֹּל.   oseh shalom uvorei et hakol.

Blessed are You, יהוה, sovereign of all creation,
creator of light and former of darkness,
maker of peace and creator of all.

אֵל אָדוֹן עַל כָּל הַמַּעֲשִׂים,   El adon al kol hama·asim
בָּרוּךְ וּמְבֹרָךְ בְּפִי כָּל נְשָׁמָה.   Baruch um'vorach befi kol haneshama
גָּדְלוֹ וְטוּבוֹ מָלֵא עוֹלָם,   Godlo vetuvo maleh olam
דַּעַת וּתְבוּנָה סֹבְבִים אוֹתוֹ.   Da·at u'tvuna sovevim oto

הַמִּתְגָּאֶה עַל חַיּוֹת הַקֹּדֶשׁ   Hamitga·eh al chayot hakodesh
וְנֶהְדָּר בְּכָבוֹד עַל הַמֶּרְכָּבָה.   Venehedar bechavod al hamerkava
זְכוּת וּמִישׁוֹר לִפְנֵי כִסְאוֹ,   Zchut u'mishor lifnei kis'oh
חֶסֶד וְרַחֲמִים לִפְנֵי כְבוֹדוֹ.   Chesed verachamim lifnei kvodo.

טוֹבִים מְאוֹרוֹת שֶׁבָּרָא אֱלֹהֵינוּ,   Tovim me·orot she'bara Eloheinu,
יְצָרָם בְּדַעַת בְּבִינָה וּבְהַשְׂכֵּל.   Yetzaram beda·at bevinah u'vhaskel.
כֹּחַ וּגְבוּרָה נָתַן בָּהֶם,   Ko·ach u'gvura natan bahem
לִהְיוֹת מוֹשְׁלִים בְּקֶרֶב תֵּבֵל.   Lihiyot moshlim bekerev tevel.

מְלֵאִים זִיו וּמְפִיקִים נֹגַהּ,   Mele·im ziv u'mefikim noga
נָאֶה זִיוָם בְּכָל הָעוֹלָם.   Na·eh zivam bechol ha·olam.
שְׂמֵחִים בְּצֵאתָם וְשָׂשִׂים בְּבוֹאָם,   Smechim betzetam vesasim bevo·am
עֹשִׂים בְּאֵימָה רְצוֹן קוֹנָם.   Osim be·emah retzon konam.

פְּאֵר וְכָבוֹד נוֹתְנִים לִשְׁמוֹ,   Pe·er vechavod notnim lishmo
צָהֳלָה וְרִנָּה לְזֵכֶר מַלְכוּתוֹ.   Tzohola verina lezecher malchuto
קָרָא לַשֶּׁמֶשׁ וַיִּזְרַח אוֹר,   Kara lashemesh vayizrach or
רָאָה, וְהִתְקִין צוּרַת הַלְּבָנָה.   Ra·ah vehitkin tzurat halevana.

שֶׁבַח נוֹתְנִים לוֹ   Shevach notnim lo
כָּל צְבָא מָרוֹם,   kol tzeva marom
תִּפְאֶרֶת וּגְדֻלָּה,   Tiferet u'gdula
שְׂרָפִים וְאוֹפַנִּים   serafim v'ofanim
וְחַיּוֹת הַקֹּדֶשׁ.   v'chayot hakodesh.

A gentle Lord of all that is.
Blessed and loved by each soul alive.
Great and good You fill all space.
Delight there is in knowing You.

How you transcend all holy life,
Which bears You high above any throne.
Z'khut and equity radiate from You
Hesed and compassion the worlds reflect.

The stars and planets You made to give light:
You formed them all conscious, all worthy and wise.
Knowledge and power You gave them to shine.
Like powerful assistants they serve You in space.

Much light and energy they radiate forth.
No place is untouched by their gentle rays.
So joyful their path is, so happy their course.
Enroute to fulfill their Creator's command.

Praising Your glory, they honor Your name,
Singing Your Majesty's anthem of joy.
Quietly suns shine to answer Your call.
Reflections of moonlight change size at Your word.

Seraphim, angels, and all heavenly hosts,
They praise You in concert with *S'firot* on high!
All elements mingle their harmonious tune
Nature and mankind in rhythm provide.

(translation: R' Zalman Schachter-Shalomi z"l)

קָדוֹשׁ, קָדוֹשׁ, קָדוֹשׁ
יהוה צְבָאוֹת,
מְלֹא כָל הָאָרֶץ כְּבוֹדוֹ.
בָּרוּךְ כְּבוֹד יהוה מִמְּקוֹמוֹ.

Kadosh, kadosh, kadosh
יהוה tzeva·ot
M'lo chol ha·aretz k'vodo.
Baruch k'vod יהוה mimkomo.

> Holy, holy, holy is the Lord God of mine.
> All the earth is full of God's glory.
> Blessed is the glory of יהוה in God's place!

תִּתְבָּרַךְ צוּרֵנוּ מַלְכֵּנוּ וְגוֹאֲלֵנוּ
בּוֹרֵא קְדוֹשִׁים, יִשְׁתַּבַּח שִׁמְךָ
לָעַד מַלְכֵּנוּ, יוֹצֵר מְשָׁרְתִים,
וַאֲשֶׁר מְשָׁרְתָיו כֻּלָּם,
עוֹמְדִים בְּרוּם עוֹלָם,
וּמַשְׁמִיעִים בְּיִרְאָה יַחַד בְּקוֹל,
דִּבְרֵי אֱלֹהִים חַיִּים וּמֶלֶךְ עוֹלָם.
כֻּלָּם אֲהוּבִים, כֻּלָּם בְּרוּרִים,
כֻּלָּם גִּבּוֹרִים, וְכֻלָּם עֹשִׂים
בְּאֵימָה וּבְיִרְאָה רְצוֹן קוֹנָם. וְכֻלָּם
פּוֹתְחִים אֶת פִּיהֶם בִּקְדֻשָּׁה וּבְטָהֳרָה,
בְּשִׁירָה וּבְזִמְרָה,
וּמְבָרְכִים וּמְשַׁבְּחִים,
וּמְפָאֲרִים וּמַעֲרִיצִים,
וּמַקְדִּישִׁים וּמַמְלִיכִים.

Titbarach tzurenu malkeinu v'goaleinu
borei k'doshim, yishtabach shimcha
la-ad malkeinu, yotzer m'shartim,
va·asher m'shartav kulam,
omdim b'rum olam,
umashmi·im b'yirah yachad b'kol,
divrei Elohim chayyim umelech olam.
Kulam ahuvim, kulam b'rurim,
kulam giborim, v'chulam osim
b'eimah u·v'yirah r'tzon konam.
V'kulam potchim et pihem bikdusha
u·v'taharah, b'shirah u·v'zimrah,
u'mvarchim u'mshabchim,
u'm'fa·arim u'ma·aritzim,
umakdishim umamlichim.

> You are blessed, our Rock, our Sovereign, our Redeemer, creator of holiness.
> We praise Your name, our sovereign, creator of the heavenly lights that serve.
> All of them serve You, standing before You, proclaiming Your oneness in awe,
> our living God and sovereign of creation.
> All of them beloved; all of them clear; all of them strong;
> all of them doing Your will in awe. All of them open their mouths in holiness
> and purity, in song and in praise, sanctifying You and proclaiming Your sovereignty.

אוֹר חָדָשׁ עַל צִיּוֹן תָּאִיר
וְנִזְכֶּה כֻלָּנוּ מְהֵרָה לְאוֹרוֹ.
בָּרוּךְ אַתָּה יהוה יוֹצֵר הַמְּאוֹרוֹת.

Or chadash al tzion ta·ir
V'nizkeh chulanu m'heirah l'oro.
Baruch atah יהוה, yotzer hame·orot.

> May a new light shine upon Zion
> and may we all swiftly merit its radiance.
> Blessed are You, יהוה, Creator of the heavenly lights.

Good (Yotzer Or)

Beloved, You are good
and you wield goodness
in shaping creation

and every single day
in Your goodness
and with Your goodness

You make us new
with all created things.
You make me new.

I cling to yesterday
(who would I be
without the sorrows

that have worn grooves
into my back?) but
that's my own smallness.

You've made me new
formed me for this new day
a sapling unbowed.

The knot in my stomach
the knot in my throat —
You untie them.

Can I sit with You
for even a few minutes
before I tangle myself again?

(Rabbi Rachel Barenblat)

Ahavah Rabbah / Blessing for Love (and Torah)

Ahavah Rabbah Chant (Lach Amar Libi, from Psalm 27)

לָךְ אָמַר לִבִּי Lach amar libi
בַּקְשׁוּ פָנָי Bakshu fanai (2x)
אֶת פָּנֶיךָ, הויה Et panayich, Havayah
אֲבַקֵּשׁ Avakeish.

You called to my heart:
Come seek My face, come seek My grace.
For Your love, Source of all,
I will seek.

Full text Ahavah Rabbah

אַהֲבָה רַבָּה אֲהַבְתָּנוּ, Ahavah raba ahavtanu
יהוה אֱלֹהֵינוּ, חֶמְלָה גְדוֹלָה יהוה Eloheinu chemlah g'dolah
וִיתֵרָה חָמַלְתָּ עָלֵינוּ. v'yteirah chamalta aleinu.
אָבִינוּ מַלְכֵּנוּ, בַּעֲבוּר אֲבוֹתֵינוּ Avinu malkeinu, ba-avur avoteinu
וְאִמּוֹתֵינוּ, שֶׁבָּטְחוּ בְךָ, v'imoteinu shebat'chu vecha,
וַתְּלַמְּדֵם חֻקֵּי חַיִּים, vat'lamdeim chukei chayim
כֵּן תְּחָנֵּנוּ וּתְלַמְּדֵנוּ. kein t'choneinu ut'lamdeinu.
אָבִינוּ, הָאָב הָרַחֲמָן, הַמְרַחֵם, Avinu ha-av harachaman, ham'racheim
רַחֵם עָלֵינוּ, וְתֵן בְּלִבֵּנוּ לְהָבִין racheim aleinu v'tein b'libeinu l'havin
וּלְהַשְׂכִּיל, לִשְׁמֹעַ, לִלְמֹד וּלְלַמֵּד, ul'haskil lishmo-a lilmod ul'lameid
לִשְׁמֹר וְלַעֲשׂוֹת וּלְקַיֵּם lishmor v'la-asot ul'kayeim
אֶת כָּל דִּבְרֵי et kol divrei
תַלְמוּד תּוֹרָתֶךָ בְּאַהֲבָה. talmud Toratecha b'ahavah.

You have loved us with a great love, יהוה our God.
With great compassion you have cared for us.
Our ancestors trusted in You and learned from You laws of life.
For their sake, have mercy on us and teach us.
You are our source and our womb — be gracious with us.
Give our hearts understanding
to hear, learn, teach and do
all the words of Your teaching with love.

וְהָאֵר עֵינֵינוּ בְּתוֹרָתֶךָ,	V'ha·eir eineinu b'Toratecha
וְדַבֵּק לִבֵּנוּ בְּמִצְוֹתֶיךָ,	v'dabek libeinu b'mitzvotecha
וְיַחֵד לְבָבֵנוּ לְאַהֲבָה וּלְיִרְאָה	v'yacheid levaveinu l'ahavah ul'yirah
אֶת שְׁמֶךָ, וְלֹא נֵבוֹשׁ	et sh'mecha. V'lo neivosh
וְלֹא נִכָּלֵם וְלֹא נִכָּשֵׁל לְעוֹלָם וָעֶד.	v'lo nikaleim v'lo nikasheil le·olam va·ed.
כִּי בְשֵׁם קָדְשְׁךָ	ki v'sheim kodshecha
הַגָּדוֹל וְהַנּוֹרָא בָּטָחְנוּ,	hagadol v'hanora batachnu,
נָגִילָה וְנִשְׂמְחָה בִּישׁוּעָתֶךָ.	nagilah v'nismechah b'y'shu·atecha.

Enlighten our eyes with Your Torah; attach us to Your mitzvot.
Unite our hearts to the love and awe of Your name.
Then we shall never be shamed or humiliated, nor shall we stumble.
We will trust in Your great, wondrous and holy name.
We will rejoice and exult in Your saving power.

וַהֲבִיאֵנוּ לְשָׁלוֹם	V'havi·einu l'shalom
מֵאַרְבַּע כַּנְפוֹת הָאָרֶץ,	mei·arba kan'fot ha·aretz
וְתוֹלִיכֵנוּ קוֹמְמִיּוּת לְאַרְצֵנוּ,	v'tolicheinu komemiyut la·artzeinu,
כִּי אֵל פּוֹעֵל יְשׁוּעוֹת אָתָּה,	ki El po·eil yeshu·ot ata,
וּבָנוּ בָחַרְתָּ מִכָּל עַם וְלָשׁוֹן.	uvanu vacharta im kol am v'lashon.
וְקֵרַבְתָּנוּ לְשִׁמְךָ הַגָּדוֹל סֶלָה בֶּאֱמֶת	V'keiravtanu l'shimcha hagadol selah b'emet
לְהוֹדוֹת לְךָ וּלְיַחֶדְךָ בְּאַהֲבָה.	l'hodot lecha ul'yached'cha b'ahavah.
בָּרוּךְ אַתָּה יהוה,	Baruch atah יהוה,
הַבּוֹחֵר בְּעַמּוֹ יִשְׂרָאֵל בְּאַהֲבָה.	habocheir b'amo Yisra·el b'ahavah.

Bring us in peace from the four corners of the earth
and lead us upright to our home,
for You are the God of redemptive power
who has chosen us with all peoples.
Draw us close to Your great name in truth,
to praise You and unify Your name.
Blessed are You, יהוה, who has in love chosen Your people.

More Love (Shaker Ahavah Rabbah)

When we love not one another in daily communion
How can we love God, whom we have never seen?

Chorus:
More love! More love!
The heavens are calling, the angels are singing,
O Zion, more love, more love.

If we love one another then God is within us
And we are made whole to dance in the light.

Chorus:
More love! More love!
The heavens are calling, the angels are singing,
O Zion, more love, more love.

אַהֲבָה רַבָּה Ahavah rabbah
אַהֲבָה בַּשָּׁמַיִם, Ahavah ba-shamayim
אַהֲבָה בְּעֵינַיִם Ahavah ba-eynayim
אַהֲבָה, אַהֲבָה רַבָּה. Ahavah, ahavah rabbah.

(adapted from a Shaker hymn)

So much (Ahavah Rabbah)

Dear One, you love me so much
you give me your Torah
for argument and play
waltzing and conversation
from one life to the next.

Your Torah nourishes me,
familiar as the womb.
Wrap me tight in your Torah
like a newborn. Laugh in delight
when I learn to break free.

Your Torah lights up my eyes,
fuses my heart with my choices.
Give me just one letter
to suck like candy, like manna
changing flavor on my tongue.

Tell me a true story again
about who I used to be
or who I might yet be
— like you, always becoming
who you are becoming.

Beloved, draw me close.
I've been scattered:
melt me until we mingle.
I want to come home in you.
Choose me again. Don't stop.

(Rabbi Rachel Barenblat)

Shema

(Donna Tukel)

שְׁמַע יִשְׂרָאֵל, Sh'ma Yisra·el:
יהוה אֱלֹהֵינוּ, יהוה Eloheinu
יהוה אֶחָד. יהוה echad!

בָּרוּךְ שֵׁם כְּבוֹד (Baruch shem k'vod
מַלְכוּתוֹ לְעוֹלָם וָעֶד. malchuto l'olam va·ed.)

Hear, O Israel: יהוה is our God, יהוה is One!
(Through time and space Your glory shines, Majestic One!)

וְאָהַבְתָּ אֵת יהוה אֱלֹהֶיךָ, V'ahavta et יהוה Elohecha,
בְּכָל לְבָבְךָ, b'chol levavcha,
וּבְכָל נַפְשְׁךָ, וּבְכָל מְאֹדֶךָ. uvchol nafsh'cha, uvchol m'odecha.
וְהָיוּ הַדְּבָרִים הָאֵלֶּה, V'hayu had'varim ha·eileh,
אֲשֶׁר אָנֹכִי מְצַוְּךָ הַיּוֹם, asher anochi m'tzv'cha hayom,
עַל לְבָבֶךָ. al levavecha.
וְשִׁנַּנְתָּם לְבָנֶיךָ, וְדִבַּרְתָּ בָּם, V'shinantam levanecha, v'dibarta bam,
בְּשִׁבְתְּךָ בְּבֵיתֶךָ, וּבְלֶכְתְּךָ בַדֶּרֶךְ, b'shivt'cha b'veitecha, uv'lecht'cha vaderech,
וּבְשָׁכְבְּךָ, וּבְקוּמֶךָ. uvshochb'cha, uvkumecha.
וּקְשַׁרְתָּם לְאוֹת עַל יָדֶךָ, Ukshartam l'ot al yadecha,
וְהָיוּ לְטֹטָפֹת בֵּין עֵינֶיךָ. v'hayu l'totafot bein einecha.
וּכְתַבְתָּם עַל מְזֻזוֹת בֵּיתֶךָ Uchtavtam al m'zuzot beitecha
וּבִשְׁעָרֶיךָ. uvisharecha.

Love the One, your God, with every heartbeat, with every breath,
with every conscious act. Keep in mind the words
I command you today.
Teach them to your children, talk about them at work;
whether you are tired or you are rested.
Let them guide the work of your hands;
keep them in the forefront of your vision.
Do not leave them at the doorway, or outside your gate.

וְהָיָה אִם שָׁמֹעַ תִּשְׁמְעוּ אֶל מִצְוֹתַי,	V'haya im shamoa tishm'u el-mitzvotai,
אֲשֶׁר אָנֹכִי מְצַוֶּה אֶתְכֶם הַיּוֹם, לְאַהֲבָה	asher anochi m'tzaveh etchem hayom, l'ahavah et יהוה eloheichem ulovdo,
אֶת יהוה אֱלֹהֵיכֶם וּלְעָבְדוֹ,	
בְּכָל לְבַבְכֶם וּבְכָל נַפְשְׁכֶם.	b'chol l'vavchem uvchol nafsh'chem.
וְנָתַתִּי מְטַר אַרְצְכֶם בְּעִתּוֹ,	V'natati m'tararotz'chem b'ito,
יוֹרֶה וּמַלְקוֹשׁ, וְאָסַפְתָּ דְגָנֶךָ	yoreh umalkosh, v'asafta d'ganecha
וְתִירֹשְׁךָ וְיִצְהָרֶךָ. וְנָתַתִּי עֵשֶׂב בְּשָׂדְךָ	v'tirosh·cha v'yitz·harecha. V'natati esev b'sadcha
לִבְהֶמְתֶּךָ, וְאָכַלְתָּ וְשָׂבָעְתָּ.	liv'hemtecha, v'achalta v'savata.
הִשָּׁמְרוּ לָכֶם פֶּן יִפְתֶּה לְבַבְכֶם,	Hisham'ru lachem pen yifteh l'vavchem,
וְסַרְתֶּם וַעֲבַדְתֶּם אֱלֹהִים אֲחֵרִים	v'sartem v'avadtem elohim acheirim
וְהִשְׁתַּחֲוִיתֶם לָהֶם.	v'hishtachavitem lahem.
וְחָרָה אַף יהוה בָּכֶם,	V'chara af יהוה bachem,
וְעָצַר אֶת הַשָּׁמַיִם וְלֹא יִהְיֶה מָטָר,	v'atzar et-hashamayim v'lo yihyeh matar,
וְהָאֲדָמָה לֹא תִתֵּן אֶת יְבוּלָהּ;	v'ha·adamah lo titen et-y'vulah;
וַאֲבַדְתֶּם מְהֵרָה מֵעַל הָאָרֶץ הַטֹּבָה	v'avadtem m'heirah me·al ha·aretz hatovah
אֲשֶׁר יהוה נֹתֵן לָכֶם.	asher יהוה notein lachem.
וְשַׂמְתֶּם אֶת דְּבָרַי אֵלֶּה עַל לְבַבְכֶם	V'samtem et-d'varai eileh al l'vavchem
וְעַל נַפְשְׁכֶם, וּקְשַׁרְתֶּם אֹתָם	v'alnafsh'chem, ukshartem otam
לְאוֹת עַל יֶדְכֶם,	l'ot al yedchem,
וְהָיוּ לְטוֹטָפֹת בֵּין עֵינֵיכֶם.	v'hayu l'totafot bein-eineichem.
וְלִמַּדְתֶּם אֹתָם אֶת בְּנֵיכֶם לְדַבֵּר בָּם,	V'limadtem otam et b'neichem l'dabeir bam,
בְּשִׁבְתְּךָ בְּבֵיתֶךָ, וּבְלֶכְתְּךָ בַדֶּרֶךְ,	b'shivt'cha b'veitecha, uvlecht'cha vaderech,
וּבְשָׁכְבְּךָ, וּבְקוּמֶךָ.	uvshochb'cha uv'kumecha.
וּכְתַבְתָּם עַל מְזוּזוֹת בֵּיתֶךָ	Uchtavtam al m'zuzot beitecha
וּבִשְׁעָרֶיךָ. לְמַעַן יִרְבּוּ יְמֵיכֶם וִימֵי	uvisharecha. L'ma·an yirbu y'meichem vimei
בְנֵיכֶם עַל הָאֲדָמָה אֲשֶׁר נִשְׁבַּע יהוה	v'neichem al ha·adamah asher nishba יהוה
לַאֲבֹתֵיכֶם לָתֵת לָהֶם,	la·avoteichem lateit lahem,
כִּימֵי הַשָּׁמַיִם עַל הָאָרֶץ.	kimei hashamayim al ha·aretz.

How good it will be when you really listen and hear My directions which I give you today, to love יהוה who is your God and to act godly with feeling and inspiration. Your earthly needs will be met at the right time, appropriate to the season. You will reap what you have planted for your delight and health. Also your animals will have ample feed. All of you will eat and be content.

Be careful—watch out! Don't let your cravings delude you; don't become alienated; don't let your cravings become your gods; don't debase yourself to them because the God-sense within you will become distorted. Heaven will be shut to you, grace will not descend, Earth will not yield her produce. Your rushing will destroy you! And Earth will not be able to recover her good balance in which God's gifts manifest.

(translation: R' Zalman Schachter-Shalomi z"l)

Listen Up Y'all / An interpretive version of וְהָיָה אִם שָׁמֹעַ

"Listen up, y'all," says Shekhinah
who looks today like a teacher
in a corduroy dress and sedate boots.

"Let the smartphone rest a bit,
or learn how to hear My voice
coming through its speaker.

Let your love for Me well up
like unexpected tears. Everyone serves
something: give your life to Me.

Let the channel of your heart open
and My abundance will pour through.
But if you prefer profit, if you pretend —

if you're not real with Me
your life will feel hollow
and your heart be embittered.

I won't punish you; I won't need to.
Your hollowness will be punishment enough,
and the world will suffer for it.

So let My words twine around your arm,
and shine like a headlamp
between your eyes to light your way.

Teach them to everyone you meet.
Write them at the end of your emails
and on your business cards.

Then you'll remember how to live
with the flow of all that is holy —
you'll have heaven right here on earth.

(Rabbi Rachel Barenblat)

וַיֹּאמֶר יהוה אֶל מֹשֶׁה לֵּאמֹר. Vayomer יהוה el-Moshe leimor:
דַּבֵּר אֶל בְּנֵי יִשְׂרָאֵל וְאָמַרְתָּ אֲלֵהֶם, Dabeir el-b'nei Yisra·el v'amarta aleihem,
וְעָשׂוּ לָהֶם צִיצִת עַל כַּנְפֵי בִגְדֵיהֶם v'asu lahem tzitzit al kanfei bigdeihem
לְדֹרֹתָם; וְנָתְנוּ עַל צִיצִת הַכָּנָף ledorotam; v'natnu al tzitzit hakanaf
פְּתִיל תְּכֵלֶת. וְהָיָה לָכֶם לְצִיצִת, p'til t'cheilet. V'yaha lachem l'tzitzit,
וּרְאִיתֶם אֹתוֹ, וּזְכַרְתֶּם אֶת כָּל uritem oto, uzchartem et kol
מִצְוֹת יהוה, וַעֲשִׂיתֶם אֹתָם, mitzvot יהוה va·asitem otam.
וְלֹא תָתוּרוּ אַחֲרֵי לְבַבְכֶם V'lo taturu acharei levavchem
וְאַחֲרֵי עֵינֵיכֶם, אֲשֶׁר אַתֶּם זֹנִים v'acharei eineichem, asher atem zonim
אַחֲרֵיהֶם. לְמַעַן תִּזְכְּרוּ וַעֲשִׂיתֶם אֶת achareihem. Lma·an tizkiru v'asitem et
כָּל מִצְוֹתָי, וִהְיִיתֶם קְדֹשִׁים לֵאלֹהֵיכֶם. kol mitzvotai, v'hiyitem k'doshim le·eloheichem.
אֲנִי יהוה אֱלֹהֵיכֶם, Ani יהוה eloheichem,
אֲשֶׁר הוֹצֵאתִי אֶתְכֶם מֵאֶרֶץ מִצְרַיִם, asher hotzeiti et·chem mei·eretz Mitzrayim,
לִהְיוֹת לָכֶם לֵאלֹהִים, liyot lachem le-Elohim:
אֲנִי יהוה אֱלֹהֵיכֶם. Ani יהוה eloheichem.

ה׳ Who Is said to Moshe:
"Speak, telling the *Yisrael* folks to make *tzitzit*
on the corners of their garments,
so they will have generations to follow them.
On each *tzitzit*-tassel let them set a blue thread.
Glance at it and in your seeing
remember all of the other directives of ה׳ who Is,
and act on them!
This way you will not be led astray,
craving to see and want,
and then prostitute yourself for your cravings.
This way you will be mindful to actualize my directions
for becoming dedicated to your God,
to be aware that I AM ה׳ who is your God —
the One who freed you from the oppression
in order to God you.
I am ה׳ your God."
This way you will be mindful to actualize my directions
for becoming dedicated to your God;
to be aware that I am your God,
the one who freed you from the oppression
in order to be your God. I am Adonai your God.
That is the truth!

(translation: R' Zalman Schachter-Shalomi z"l)

Ge·ulah / Blessing for Redemption

Short Ge·ulah Chant

עָזִּי וְזִמְרָת יָהּ וַיְהִי־לִי לִישׁוּעָה. Ozi v'zimrat Yah, vay'hi li l'yshu·ah.

My strength is in Your song, and You will be my salvation.

(Photograph by Ze'ev Barkan)

Full Text Ge·ulah

אֱמֶת וְיַצִּיב וְנָכוֹן וְקַיָּם וְיָשָׁר	Emet v'yatziv v'nakhon v'kayam v'yashar
וְנֶאֱמָן וְאָהוּב וְחָבִיב וְנֶחְמָד	v'ne·eman v'ahuv v'chaviv v'nechmad
וְנָעִים וְנוֹרָא וְאַדִּיר וּמְתֻקָּן	v'na·im v'nora v'adir um'tukan um'kubal
וּמְקֻבָּל וְטוֹב וְיָפֶה הַדָּבָר הַזֶּה	v'tov v'yafeh hadavar hazeh
עָלֵינוּ לְעוֹלָם וָעֶד.	aleinu l'olam va·ed.
אֱמֶת אֱלֹהֵי עוֹלָם מַלְכֵּנוּ	Emet Elohei olam malkeinu
צוּר יַעֲקֹב, מָגֵן יִשְׁעֵנוּ,	tzur Ya·akov, magein yisheinu,
לְדֹר וָדֹר הוּא קַיָּם, וּשְׁמוֹ קַיָּם,	l'dor vador hu kayam, u'shmo kayam,
וְכִסְאוֹ נָכוֹן, וּמַלְכוּתוֹ וֶאֱמוּנָתוֹ	v'khis'o nakhon, u'malkhuto ve·emunato
לָעַד קַיָּמֶת. וּדְבָרָיו חָיִים	la·ad kayamet. Ud'varav chayim
וְקַיָּמִים, נֶאֱמָנִים וְנֶחֱמָדִים לָעַד	v'kayamim, ne·emanim v'nechemadim la·ad
וּלְעוֹלְמֵי עוֹלָמִים.	u'l'olmei olamim.
עַל אֲבוֹתֵינוּ וְעָלֵינוּ,	Al avoteinu v'aleinu,
עַל בָּנֵינוּ וְעַל דּוֹרוֹתֵינוּ,	al baneinu v'al doroteinu,
וְעַל כָּל דּוֹרוֹת	v'al kol dorot
זֶרַע יִשְׂרָאֵל עֲבָדֶיךָ.	zera Yisra·el avadekha.

True and enduring,
right and real, upright and faithful,
beloved and cherished, desired and pleasant, awesome and mighty,
healing and revealed, good and beautiful is this truth for us for all time.

It is true that You are our sovereign, rock of Jacob and shield of our deliverance.
From generation to generation You endure and Your name endures,
and Your throne is confirmed, and Your sovereignty and faithfulness endure forever.
Your words live and endure, faithful and desirable forever in all worlds.
For our ancestors as for us, and for our children and our generations and all
generations to come: we seek to serve You.

עַל הָרִאשׁוֹנִים וְעַל הָאַחֲרוֹנִים, Al harishonim v'al ha·acharonim,
דָּבָר טוֹב וְקַיָּם לְעוֹלָם וָעֶד, davar tov v'kayam l'olam va·ed,
אֱמֶת וֶאֱמוּנָה חֹק וְלֹא יַעֲבֹר. emet v'emuna chok v'lo ya·avor.
אֱמֶת שָׁאַתָּה הוּא יהוה אֱלֹהֵינוּ Emet sha·atah hu יהוה Eloheinu
וֵאלֹהֵי אֲבוֹתֵינוּ, v'Eilohei avoteinu,
מַלְכֵּנוּ מֶלֶךְ אֲבוֹתֵינוּ, malkeinu melech avoteinu,
גֹּאֲלֵנוּ גֹּאֵל אֲבוֹתֵינוּ, go·aleinu go·eil avoteinu,
יוֹצְרֵנוּ צוּר יְשׁוּעָתֵינוּ, yotz'reinu tzur y'shu·ateinu,
פּוֹדֵנוּ וּמַצִּילֵנוּ מֵעוֹלָם שְׁמֶךָ, podeinu u'matzileinu mei·olam sh'mekha,
אֵין אֱלֹהִים זוּלָתֶךָ. ein Elohim zulatekha.

From the first to the last
this truth is good and enduring forever,
true and faithful,
an engraved-commandment that will not pass from us.
It is true that You are our God and God of our ancestors,
Sovereign of our generations, Redeemer of our forebears,
Creator, Rock, Liberator and Saver are among Your names.
There is no God but You.

עֶזְרַת אֲבוֹתֵינוּ אַתָּה הוּא מֵעוֹלָם,	Ezrat avoteinu atah hu mei·olam,
מָגֵן וּמוֹשִׁיעַ לִבְנֵיהֶם אַחֲרֵיהֶם	magein u'moshi·a liv'neihem achareihem
בְּכָל דּוֹר וָדוֹר.	b'khol dor va'dor.
בְּרוּם עוֹלָם מוֹשָׁבֶךָ,	B'rum olam moshavekha,
וּמִשְׁפָּטֶיךָ וְצִדְקָתְךָ עַד אַפְסֵי אָרֶץ.	u'mishpatekha v'tzidkat'kha ad afsei aretz.
אַשְׁרֵי אִישׁ שֶׁיִּשְׁמַע לְמִצְוֹתֶיךָ,	Ashrei ish she'yishma l'mitzvotekha,
וְתוֹרָתְךָ וּדְבָרְךָ יָשִׂים עַל לִבּוֹ.	v'torat'kha u'dvar'kha yasim al libo.
אֱמֶת אַתָּה הוּא אָדוֹן לְעַמֶּךָ,	Emet atah hu adon l'amekha,
וּמֶלֶךְ גִּבּוֹר לָרִיב רִיבָם.	u'melech gibor lariv rivam.
אֱמֶת אַתָּה הוּא רִאשׁוֹן	Emet atah hu rishon
וְאַתָּה הוּא אַחֲרוֹן,	v'atah hu acharon,
וּמִבַּלְעָדֶיךָ אֵין לָנוּ מֶלֶךְ	u'mibal·adekha ein lanu melech
גּוֹאֵל וּמוֹשִׁיעַ.	go·eil u'moshi·a.
מִמִּצְרַיִם גְּאַלְתָּנוּ יְיָ אֱלֹהֵינוּ,	Mi'mitzrayim g'altanu Adonai Eloheinu,
וּמִבֵּית עֲבָדִים פְּדִיתָנוּ.	u'mibeit avadim p'ditanu.
וְיַם סוּף בָּקַעְתָּ, וְזֵדִים טִבַּעְתָּ,	V'Yam Suf bakata, v'zeidim tibata,
וִידִידִים הֶעֱבַרְתָּ,	vi'didim he·evarta,
וַיְכַסּוּ מַיִם צָרֵיהֶם,	va'y'khasu mayim tzareihem,
אֶחָד מֵהֶם לֹא נוֹתָר.	echad meihem lo notar.
עַל זֹאת שִׁבְּחוּ אֲהוּבִים וְרוֹמְמוּ אֵל,	Al zot shib'chu ahuvim v'rom'mu El,
וְנָתְנוּ יְדִידִים זְמִרוֹת שִׁירוֹת וְתִשְׁבָּחוֹת,	v'nat'nu y'didim z'mirot shirot v'tishbachot,
בְּרָכוֹת וְהוֹדָאוֹת,	b'rachot v'hoda·ot,
לְמֶלֶךְ אֵל חַי וְקַיָּם,	l'melech El chai v'kayam,
רָם וְנִשָּׂא, גָּדוֹל וְנוֹרָא,	ram v'nisa, gadol v'nora,
מַשְׁפִּיל גֵּאִים, וּמַגְבִּיהַּ שְׁפָלִים,	mashpil gei·im, u'magbi·ha sh'falim,
מוֹצִיא אֲסִירִים, וּפוֹדֶה עֲנָוִים,	motzi asirim, u'fodeh anavim,
וְעוֹזֵר דַּלִּים,	v'ozeir dalim,
וְעוֹנֶה לְעַמּוֹ בְּעֵת שַׁוְּעָם אֵלָיו.	v'oneh l'amo b'eit shav·am eilav.
תְּהִלּוֹת לְאֵל עֶלְיוֹן,	T'hilot l'El elyon,
בָּרוּךְ הוּא וּמְבֹרָךְ.	baruch hu u'mvorach.
מֹשֶׁה וּמִרְיָם וּבְנֵי יִשְׂרָאֵל	Moshe u'Miriam u'vnei Yisra·el
לְךָ עָנוּ שִׁירָה	l'kha anu shirah
בְּשִׂמְחָה רַבָּה וְאָמְרוּ כֻלָּם.	b'simchah raba v'amru khulam:

You have been the help relied-on by our forehears,
Shield and Deliverer to their children after them in every generation.
You inhabit the heights of the universe;
Your judgments and righteousness extend to the ends of the earth.
Fortunate is the one who is connected to Your mitzvot
and who takes Your Torah and teachings to heart.
Truly You are Sovereign of Your people
and You are mighty in defending us.
Truly You are first and You are last,
and beside You we have no ruler, redeemer, or savior.
From Egypt You redeemed us, יהוה our God;
from the house of bondage You liberated us.
You split the Sea of Reeds and drowned the wicked
and enabled Your beloved ones to pass through
while the waters covered their enemies: not one remained.
Because of this,
Your beloved ones offered hymns, songs, and praises,
blessings and thanksgiving
to the One, the Almighty, living and enduring,
exalted and uplifted, great and awesome,
Who humbles the prideful and raises the lowly,
Who frees the captive and redeems the humble
and helps the impoverished.
You help Your people when we cry out.
Praises to the Most High who is blessed!

Moshe and Miriam and the children of Israel
sang out in joy to you, and they all proclaimed:

The Water is Wide

The water is wide, I cannot get o'er
And neither have I wings to fly
Give me a boat that can carry two
And both shall row, my love and I.

מִי כָמֹכָה בָּאֵלִם יהוה, Mi chamocha ba·eilim יהוה,
מִי כָּמֹכָה נֶאְדָּר בַּקֹּדֶשׁ, mi camocha nedar bakodesh,
נוֹרָא תְהִלֹּת עֹשֵׂה פֶלֶא. nora tehilot oseh feleh.

שִׁירָה חֲדָשָׁה שִׁבְּחוּ גְאוּלִים לְשִׁמְךָ Shirah chadasha shib'chu ge·ulim
עַל שְׂפַת הַיָּם, l'shimcha al s'fat hayam,
יַחַד כֻּלָּם הוֹדוּ וְהִמְלִיכוּ וְאָמְרוּ: yachad kulam hodu v'himlichu v'amru:
יהוה יִמְלֹךְ לְעֹלָם וָעֶד. יהוה yimloch l'olam va·ed.

צוּר יִשְׂרָאֵל, Tzur Yisra·el,
קוּמָה בְּעֶזְרַת יִשְׂרָאֵל, kumah b'ezrat Yisra·el,
וּפְדֵה כִנְאֻמֶךָ יְהוּדָה וְיִשְׂרָאֵל. ufdei chinumecha y'hudah v'Yisra·el.
גֹּאֲלֵנוּ יהוה צְבָאוֹת שְׁמוֹ, Go·aleinu יהוה tz'va·ot shemo,
קְדוֹשׁ יִשְׂרָאֵל. k'dosh Yisra·el.
בָּרוּךְ אַתָּה יהוה גָּאַל יִשְׂרָאֵל. Baruch atah יהוה ga·al Yisra·el.

Who is like You among the gods, יהוה?
Who is like You, awesome and doing wonders?
On the shores of the sea,
the redeemed sang a new song of praise to Your name.
As one,
they thanked You and declared You ruler,
crying,
"יהוה will reign forever and ever."

Rock of Israel,
arise and come to the aid of Israel!
Redeem us as You have promised.
We know you as the God of hosts;
sanctify us.
Blessed are You, יהוה, Who redeems Your people Israel.

Journey

between
a pillar of cloud
and a pillar of fire
the sea yawns
birth canal
labyrinth
blood-painted door

we enter joyful
that the future is just ahead

we enter afraid
of what pursues us

we enter
present with not knowing

we have escaped slavery
just barely
someone bought our freedom
we're not sure who
ancestors
children
prophets
the all-weaver
the angel of death

to either side
the water is mirrors
is windows
is a view of the deep

just ahead
is darkness
is a light shining
is the sound of singing
and the pounding of feet

(Rabbi Jill Hammer)

Amidah

   In this siddur there are two versions of the Shabbat Amidah, the standing prayer that is at the heart of every Jewish service. In the morning service there is a Full-Text Shabbat Amidah; in the Mincha (afternoon) service there is a Contemplative Shabbat Amidah. If you prefer the Contemplative version, it is on p. 113.

Open Your Gate

My God, life of all worlds, constantly renewing creation:
Open Your gate of prayer, that our hearts and souls may arise into Your light.
Open Your gate of vision, that we may see our path clear.
Open Your gate of forgiveness, that we may return to You.
Open my mouth and my lips will declare Your praise.

(Rabbi David Evan Markus)

Full Text *Amidah*

אֲדֹנָי שְׂפָתַי תִּפְתָּח Adonai s'fatai tiftach
וּפִי יַגִּיד תְּהִלָּתֶךָ. ufi yagid t'hilatecha.

Eternal God, open my lips
that my mouth may declare Your praise.

Avot V'imahot / Ancestors

בָּרוּךְ אַתָּה יהוה Baruch atah יהוה
אֱלֹהֵינוּ וֵאלֹהֵי אֲבוֹתֵינוּ וְאִמּוֹתֵינוּ, Eloheinu v'Elohei avoteinu v'imoteinu,
אֱלֹהֵי אַבְרָהָם, אֱלֹהֵי יִצְחָק, Elohei Avraham, Elohei Yitzchak,
וֵאלֹהֵי יַעֲקֹב, V'Elohei Ya·akov,

some omit

אֱלֹהֵי שָׂרָה, אֱלֹהֵי רִבְקָה, Elohei Sarah, Elohei Rivkah,
אֱלֹהֵי רָחֵל, וֵאלֹהֵי לֵאָה. Elohei Rachel, v'Elohei Lei·ah.

הָאֵל הַגָּדוֹל הַגִּבּוֹר וְהַנּוֹרָא, Ha-El hagadol hagibor v'hanora
אֵל עֶלְיוֹן, גּוֹמֵל חֲסָדִים טוֹבִים, El elyon, gomeil chasadim tovim
וְקוֹנֵה הַכֹּל, v'koneih hakol
וְזוֹכֵר חַסְדֵי אָבוֹת וְאִמָּהוֹת, v'zocheir chasdei avot v'imahot,
וּמֵבִיא גוֹאֵל לִבְנֵי בְנֵיהֶם, umeivi go·eil livnei v'neihem
לְמַעַן שְׁמוֹ בְּאַהֲבָה. l'ma·an sh'mo b'ahavah.

Blessed are You,
Yah our God and God of our ancestors,
God of Abraham, God of Isaac, God of Jacob;
God of Sarah, God of Rebecca, God of Rachel and God of Leah;
the great, mighty, and awesome God,
God on high, who does deeds of loving kindness,
who is the Source of all,
and who remembers the steadfast love of our ancestors,
who lovingly brings redemption to their children's children
for Your name's sake.

> *During the Ten Days of Repentance (between Rosh Hashanah and Yom Kippur):*
>
> זָכְרֵנוּ לְחַיִּים, Zochreinu l'chayim,
> מֶלֶךְ חָפֵץ בַּחַיִּים, melech chafeitz bachayim,
> וְכָתְבֵנוּ בְּסֵפֶר הַחַיִּים, v'chotveinu b'sefer hachayim,
> לְמַעַנְךָ, אֱלֹהִים חַיִּים. l'ma·ancha, Elohim chayim.
>
> Remember us for life, Sovereign who chooses life, and inscribe us
> in the book of life for Your sake, God of life.

מֶלֶךְ עוֹזֵר וּמוֹשִׁיעַ וּמָגֵן. Melech ozeir umoshi·ah umagen.
בָּרוּךְ אַתָּה, יהוה, מָגֵן אַבְרָהָם Baruch atah יהוה, magein Avraham
some omit
וְעֶזְרַת שָׂרָה. v'ezrat Sarah.

Ruler, Helper, Redeemer, and Protector,
blessed are You, Abraham's shield and Sarah's strength.

Gevurot / Strength

אַתָּה גִבּוֹר לְעוֹלָם, יהוה, Atah gibor l'olam יהוה,
מְחַיֵּה מֵתִים אַתָּה, רַב לְהוֹשִׁיעַ. m'chayeih meitim atah rav l'hoshi·a.

Summer:
מוֹרִיד הַטָּל. Morid hatal.

Winter:
מַשִּׁיב הָרוּחַ וּמוֹרִיד הַגֶּשֶׁם. Mashiv haruach umorid hagashem.

You are our eternal strength, יהוה.
Your saving power gives life that transcends death.

Summer: You bring the dew of the field.
Winter: You cause the winds to blow & the rains to fall.

AMIDAH

מְכַלְכֵּל חַיִּים בְּחֶסֶד, M'chalkeil chayim b'chesed,
מְחַיֵּה מֵתִים בְּרַחֲמִים רַבִּים, m'chayeih meitim b'rachamim rabim,
סוֹמֵךְ נוֹפְלִים, וְרוֹפֵא חוֹלִים, someich noflim, v'rofei cholim,
וּמַתִּיר אֲסוּרִים, umatir asurim,
וּמְקַיֵּם אֱמוּנָתוֹ לִישֵׁנֵי עָפָר. umkayeim emunato lisheinei afar.
מִי כָמוֹךָ בַּעַל גְּבוּרוֹת Mi chamocha, ba·al g'vurot;
וּמִי דּוֹמֶה לָּךְ, umi domeh-lach?
מֶלֶךְ מֵמִית וּמְחַיֶּה melech meimit umchayeh,
וּמַצְמִיחַ יְשׁוּעָה. umatzmi·ach y'shu·ah.

You sustain the living with kindness,
in Your great mercy You bestow eternal life.
You support the fallen, heal the sick,
and free the captive.
You keep Your faith with us beyond life and death.
There is none like You, our Source of strength,
the ruler of life and death, the Source of our redemption.

During the Ten Days of Repentance (between Rosh Hashanah and Yom Kippur):

מִי כָמוֹךָ אַב הָרַחֲמִים, Mi chamocha av harachamim,
זוֹכֵר יְצוּרָיו לְחַיִּים בְּרַחֲמִים. zocheir y'tzurav l'chayim b'rachamim.

Who is like You, Merciful Parent? You remember us for life in compassion!

וְנֶאֱמָן אַתָּה לְהַחֲיוֹת מֵתִים. V'ne·eman atah l'hachayot meitim.
בָּרוּךְ אַתָּה, יהוה, מְחַיֵּה הַמֵּתִים. Baruch atah, יהוה, m'chayeih hameitim.

Our faith is with You, the God Who brings eternal life.
Blessed are You, יהוה, Who gives life which transcends death.

AMIDAH

Kidushat HaShem Option I / Sanctification of God's Name

(In the presence of a minyan, recite the following Kedushah:)

נְקַדֵּשׁ אֶת שִׁמְךָ בָּעוֹלָם,	N'kadeish et shimcha ba·olam;
כְּשֵׁם שֶׁמַּקְדִּישִׁים אוֹתוֹ	k'sheim shemakdishim oto
בִּשְׁמֵי מָרוֹם,	bishmei marom,
כַּכָּתוּב עַל יַד נְבִיאֶךָ:	kakatuv al yad n'vi·echa:
וְקָרָא זֶה אֶל זֶה וְאָמַר:	v'kara zeh elzeh v'amar:
קָדוֹשׁ, קָדוֹשׁ, קָדוֹשׁ,	**Kadosh kadosh kadosh,**
יהוה צְבָאוֹת,	**יהוה tz'vaot,**
מְלֹא כָל הָאָרֶץ כְּבוֹדוֹ.	**m'lo chol ha·aretz k'vodo.**
לְעֻמָּתָם בָּרוּךְ יֹאמֵרוּ:	L'umatam baruch yomeru:
בָּרוּךְ כְּבוֹד יהוה מִמְּקוֹמוֹ.	**baruch k'vod יהוה mimkomo.**
וּבְדִבְרֵי קָדְשְׁךָ כָּתוּב לֵאמֹר:	Uv'divrei kodesha katuv lemor:
יִמְלֹךְ יהוה לְעוֹלָם, אֱלֹהַיִךְ צִיּוֹן,	**Yimloch יהוה l'olam, Elohayich Tziyon,**
לְדֹר וָדֹר, הַלְלוּיָהּ.	**ledor vador, hal'lu·Yah.**
לְדוֹר וָדוֹר נַגִּיד גָּדְלֶךָ,	L'dor vador nagid godlecha,
וּלְנֵצַח נְצָחִים קְדֻשָּׁתְךָ נַקְדִּישׁ,	ulneitzach n'tzachim k'dushatcha nakdish;
וְשִׁבְחֲךָ, אֱלֹהֵינוּ,	b'shivchacha, Eloheinu,
מִפִּינוּ לֹא יָמוּשׁ לְעוֹלָם וָעֶד,	mipinu lo yamush l'olam va·ed,
כִּי אֵל מֶלֶךְ גָּדוֹל וְקָדוֹשׁ אָתָּה.	ki El melech gadol v'kadosh atah.
*בָּרוּךְ אַתָּה יהוה, הָאֵל הַקָּדוֹשׁ.	*Baruch atah יהוה, ha·El hakadosh.

> *During the Ten Days of Repentance:
> בָּרוּךְ אַתָּה, יהוה, הַמֶּלֶךְ הַקָּדוֹשׁ. Baruch atah, יהוה, ha·Melech hakadosh.

(In the absence of a minyan, use this short Kedushah instead:)

אַתָּה קָדוֹשׁ וְשִׁמְךָ קָדוֹשׁ,	Atah kadosh v'shimcha kadosh
וּקְדוֹשִׁים בְּכָל יוֹם יְהַלְלוּךָ סֶּלָה.	ukdoshim b'chol yom y'hal'lucha selah.
*בָּרוּךְ אַתָּה יהוה, הָאֵל הַקָּדוֹשׁ.	*Baruch atah יהוה, ha·El hakadosh.

> *During the Ten Days of Repentance:
> בָּרוּךְ אַתָּה, יהוה, הַמֶּלֶךְ הַקָּדוֹשׁ. Baruch atah, יהוה, ha·Melech hakadosh.

May Your name be sanctified in the world
as the angels sanctify
it in the heavens above.
As Your prophet wrote,
they cry out to one another:

**Holy, holy, holy
is יהוה Tzevaot!
The whole earth is filled with Your glory!**

And those who bless You say:
Blessed is the glory of יהוה from God's place.

And in Your holy words it is written:
**May יהוה, your God, O Zion,
rule eternally from generation to generation. Hallelujah!**

May each generation speak of Your greatness to the next.
For all eternity, may we sanctify Your holiness.
May Your praise, our God,
never depart from our lips,
for You are our great and holy God.
*Blessed are You, יהוה, the holy God.

*During the Ten Days of Repentance: Blessed are You, יהוה, the holy King.

(In the absence of a *minyan*, use this short kedushah instead:)

You are holy, and Your name is holy,
and holy ones praise You always.
*Blessed are You, יהוה, the holy God.

*During the Ten Days of Repentance: Blessed are You, יהוה, the holy King.

Kidushat HaShem Option II / Sanctification of God's Name

(In the presence of a minyan, recite the following Kedushah:)

נְקַדֵּשׁ אֶת שִׁמְךָ בָּעוֹלָם,
כְּשֵׁם שֶׁמַּקְדִּישִׁים אוֹתוֹ
בִּשְׁמֵי מָרוֹם,
כַּכָּתוּב עַל יַד נְבִיאֶךָ:
וְקָרָא זֶה אֶל זֶה וְאָמַר:

N'kadeish et shimcha ba·olam;
k'sheim shemakdishim oto
bishmei marom,
kakatuv al yad n'vi·echa:
v'kara zeh elzeh v'amar:

קָדוֹשׁ, קָדוֹשׁ, קָדוֹשׁ,
יהוה צְבָאוֹת,
מְלֹא כָל הָאָרֶץ כְּבוֹדוֹ.

Kadosh kadosh kadosh,
יהוה tz'vaot,
m'lo chol ha-aretz k'vodo.

אָז בְּקוֹל רַעַשׁ גָּדוֹל אַדִּיר וְחָזָק
מַשְׁמִיעִים קוֹל, מִתְנַשְּׂאִים לְעֻמַּת
שְׂרָפִים, לְעֻמָּתָם בָּרוּךְ יֹאמֵרוּ:

Az bakol ra·ash gadol adir v'chazak
mashmi·im kol, mitnasim l'umat
s'rafim, l'umatam baruch yomeru.

בָּרוּךְ כְּבוֹד יהוה מִמְּקוֹמוֹ.

Baruch k'vod יהוה mimkomo.

מִמְּקוֹמְךָ מַלְכֵּנוּ תוֹפִיעַ,
וְתִמְלֹךְ עָלֵינוּ, כִּי מְחַכִּים אֲנַחְנוּ לָךְ.
מָתַי תִּמְלֹךְ בְּצִיּוֹן, בְּקָרוֹב בְּיָמֵינוּ
לְעוֹלָם וָעֶד תִּשְׁכֹּן.
תִּתְגַּדַּל וְתִתְקַדַּשׁ בְּתוֹךְ יְרוּשָׁלַיִם
עִירְךָ, לְדוֹר וָדוֹר וּלְנֵצַח נְצָחִים. וְעֵינֵינוּ
תִרְאֶינָה מַלְכוּתֶךָ,
כַּדָּבָר הָאָמוּר בְּשִׁירֵי עֻזֶּךָ,
עַל יְדֵי דָוִד מְשִׁיחַ צִדְקֶךָ:
יִמְלֹךְ יהוה לְעוֹלָם, אֱלֹהַיִךְ צִיּוֹן,
לְדֹר וָדֹר, הַלְלוּיָהּ.

Mimkom'cha malkeinu tofi·a,
v'timloch aleinu, ki machakim anachnu lach.
Matai timloch b'tzion, b'karov b'yameinu
l'olam va·ed tishkon.
Titgadal v'titkadash b'toch Yerushalayim
irecha, l'dor vador u'l'netzach netzachim.
V'eineinu tireina malchutecha,
kadavar ha-amur b'shirei uzecha,
al y'dei David moshiach tzidkecha.
Yimloch יהוה l'olam, Elohayich Tziyon,
ledor vador, hal'lu·Yah.

לְדוֹר וָדוֹר נַגִּיד גָּדְלֶךָ,
וּלְנֵצַח נְצָחִים קְדֻשָּׁתְךָ נַקְדִּישׁ,
וְשִׁבְחֲךָ, אֱלֹהֵינוּ,
מִפִּינוּ לֹא יָמוּשׁ לְעוֹלָם וָעֶד,
כִּי אֵל מֶלֶךְ גָּדוֹל וְקָדוֹשׁ אָתָּה.
*בָּרוּךְ אַתָּה יהוה, הָאֵל הַקָּדוֹשׁ.

L'dor vador nagid godlecha,
ulneitzach n'tzachim k'dushatcha nakdish;
b'shivchacha, Eloheinu,
mipinu lo yamush l'olam va·ed,
ki El melech gadol v'kadosh atah.
Baruch atah, יהוה, ha·El hakadosh.

---

*During the Ten Days of Repentance:
בָּרוּךְ אַתָּה, יהוה, הַמֶּלֶךְ הַקָּדוֹשׁ. Baruch atah, יהוה, ha·Melech hakadosh.

We make Your Name holy in the world,
just as Your Name is made holy on high.
As written in the words of Your prophet,
angels call one to another,
saying:

**Holy, holy, holy
is YHVH of Hosts:
all the world fills with Your glory!**

With resounding might,
their adoring voices lifted them high up to the Seraphim.
Facing each other, they blessed saying:

Blessed is the glory of YHVH from its place!

From Your place, our Sovereign appears and reigns,
as we wait for You.
When will You reign in Zion?
Soon, in our days, may You come to dwell forever.
May Your greatness and holiness be in Jerusalem,
Your city, from generation to generation forever.
May our eyes behold Your indwelling realm,
as said in songs we sing of Your power.
By the hands of Your beloved, delivering Your righteousness:

**YHVH will reign forever:
Zion, your God of redemption, for all generations,
HalleluYah.**

Our generations will declare Your greatness,
forever sanctifying Your holiness.
Let our praise of You never leave our lips,
for You, God, are our great and holy Sovereign.
Blessed are You, YHVH, holy God.

---

*During the Ten Days of Repentance: Blessed are You, יהוה, the holy King.

AMIDAH

Kidushat HaYom Shel Shacharit / Blessing the Day - Morning Service

יִשְׂמַח מֹשֶׁה בְּמַתְּנַת חֶלְקוֹ, Yismach Moshe b'matnat chelko,
כִּי עֶבֶד נֶאֱמָן קָרָאתָ לּוֹ. ki eved ne·eman karata lo.
כְּלִיל תִּפְאֶרֶת בְּרֹאשׁוֹ נָתַתָּ לּוֹ K'lil tif·eret b'rosho natata lo
בְּעָמְדוֹ לְפָנֶיךָ עַל הַר סִינָי. b'amdo l'fanecha al Har Sinai.
וּשְׁנֵי לוּחוֹת אֲבָנִים הוֹרִיד בְּיָדוֹ, U'shnei luchot avanim horid b'yado,
וְכָתוּב בָּהֶם שְׁמִירַת שַׁבָּת. v'khatuv bahem sh'mirat Shabbat.
וְכֵן כָּתוּב בְּתוֹרָתֶךָ. V'khen katuv b'toratekha:

Moshe rejoiced in the gift of his portion,
for You called him a faithful servant.
You placed a crown of glory on his head
when he stood before You on Mount Sinai.
You gave the two tablets into his hands,
and wrote on them the mitzvah of keeping Shabbat,
and so it's written in Your Torah:

וְשָׁמְרוּ בְנֵי יִשְׂרָאֵל אֶת הַשַּׁבָּת, V'shamru v'nei Yisra·el et haShabbat,
לַעֲשׂוֹת אֶת הַשַּׁבָּת לְדֹרֹתָם בְּרִית עוֹלָם. la·asot et haShabbat l'dorotam b'rit olam.
בֵּינִי וּבֵין בְּנֵי יִשְׂרָאֵל אוֹת הִיא לְעֹלָם, Beini u-vein b'nei Yisra·el ot hi l'olam,
כִּי שֵׁשֶׁת יָמִים עָשָׂה יהוה ki sheishet yamim asah יהוה
אֶת הַשָּׁמַיִם וְאֶת הָאָרֶץ, et hashamayim v'et ha·aretz,
וּבַיּוֹם הַשְּׁבִיעִי שָׁבַת וַיִּנָּפַשׁ. u'vayom hash'vi·i shavat vayinafash.

The children of Israel shall keep Shabbat
and shall make Shabbat in all their generations:
it is a covenant for all time.
"Between Me and the children of Israel [You said] it is a sign forever!"
For in six days יהוה made the heavens and the earth,
and on the seventh day, God rested and was ensouled.

עַם מְקַדְּשֵׁי שְׁבִיעִי, Am m'kad'shei sh'vi·i,
כֻּלָּם יִשְׂבְּעוּ וְיִתְעַנְּגוּ מִטּוּבֶךָ, kulam yisb'u v'yitan'gu mituvekha,
וּבַשְּׁבִיעִי רָצִיתָ בּוֹ וְקִדַּשְׁתּוֹ, u'vash'vi·i ratzita bo v'kidashto,
חֶמְדַּת יָמִים אוֹתוֹ קָרָאתָ, chemdat yamim oto karata,
זֵכֶר לְמַעֲשֵׂה בְרֵאשִׁית. zeikher l'ma·aseh v'reishit.

The people who sanctify the seventh day
will be satisfied and delighted from Your goodness.
In the seventh day You took pleasure and made it holy. "Most desirable of days,"
You called it, in commemoration of the work of creating the world.

Kidushat HaYom Shel Mincha / Blessing the Day - Afternoon Service

אַתָּה אֶחָד וְשִׁמְךָ אֶחָד Atah echad v'shimcha echad
וּמִי כְּעַמְּךָ יִשְׂרָאֵל גּוֹי אֶחָד בָּאָרֶץ. umi k'amcha Yisra·el goy echad ba·aretz.
תִּפְאֶרֶת גְּדֻלָּה וַעֲטֶרֶת יְשׁוּעָה Tiferet g'dulah va·ateret yeshu·ah
יוֹם מְנוּחָה וּקְדֻשָּׁה לְעַמְּךָ נָתָתָּ. yom menucha uk'dushah l'amcha natata.

You are One, and Your name is One.
Who is like Your people Israel, uniquely who we are?
You have given us a day of rest and holiness;
a crown of salvation, balance and greatness.

אַבְרָהָם יָגֵל, יִצְחָק יְרַנֵּן, Avraham yagel, Yitzchak y'ranen
יַעֲקֹב וּבָנָיו יָנוּחוּ בוֹ. Ya'akov ubanav yanuchu bo.
מְנוּחַת אַהֲבָה וּנְדָבָה. M'nuchat ahavah undavah.
מְנוּחַת אֱמֶת וֶאֱמוּנָה. M'nuchat emet v'emunah.
מְנוּחַת שָׁלוֹם וְשַׁלְוָה M'nuchat shalom v'shalvah
וְהַשְׁקֵט וָבֶטַח, v'hashket vavetach,
מְנוּחָה שְׁלֵמָה שָׁאַתָּה רוֹצֶה בָּהּ. m'nuchah sh'leimah she·atah rotzeh bah.
יַכִּירוּ בָנֶיךָ וְיֵדְעוּ Yakiru baneicha viyeidu
כִּי מֵאִתְּךָ הִיא מְנוּחָתָם ki me*itcha hi m'nuchatam
וְעַל מְנוּחָתָם יַקְדִּישׁוּ אֶת שְׁמֶךָ. v'al m'nuchatam yakdisu et sh'mecha

Abraham rejoices, Isaac exults, Jacob and his descendants find rest in it:
A deep rest of love and giving, truth and faithfulness,
Peace and wholeness, security and trust –
The deep and whole rest that You desire.
Your children will recognize and know that our rest is from You,
and with and in that rest, we sanctify Your name.

AMIDAH

Kidushat HaYom / Blessing the Day continued - Morning & Afternoon

אֱלֹהֵינוּ וֵאלֹהֵי אֲבוֹתֵינוּ,　　Eloheinu veilohei avoteinu,
רְצֵה נָא בִמְנוּחָתֵנוּ,　　r'tzei na vi'mnuchateinu,
קַדְּשֵׁנוּ בְּמִצְוֹתֶיךָ　　kad'sheinu b'mitzvotekha
וְתֵן חֶלְקֵנוּ בְּתוֹרָתֶךָ,　　v'tein chelkeinu b'toratekha,
שַׂבְּעֵנוּ מִטּוּבֶךָ　　sab'einu mituvekha
וְשַׂמְּחֵנוּ בִּישׁוּעָתֶךָ,　　v'samcheinu bishu·atekha,
וְטַהֵר לִבֵּנוּ לְעָבְדְּךָ בֶּאֱמֶת,　　v'taheir libeinu l'ovd'kha be·emet,
וְהַנְחִילֵנוּ יהוה אֱלֹהֵינוּ בְּאַהֲבָה　　v'hanchileinu יהוה Eloheinu b'ahavah
וּבְרָצוֹן שַׁבַּת קָדְשֶׁךָ,　　u'vratzon Shabbat kodshekha,
וְיָנוּחוּ בוֹ כָּל יִשְׂרָאֵל מְקַדְּשֵׁי שְׁמֶךָ.　　v'yanuchu vo kol Yisra·el m'kad'shei sh'mekha.
בָּרוּךְ אַתָּה יהוה, מְקַדֵּשׁ הַשַּׁבָּת.　　Baruch atah יהוה, m'kadesh haShabbat.

God and God of our generations,
take pleasure in our rest.
Sanctify us with Your commandments
and give us our share in Your Torah.
Satisfy us with Your goodness and gladden us with Your deliverance,
and purify our hearts to serve You in truth.
Give us our inheritance, יהוה our God, in love and in pleasure: Your holy Shabbat!
And may we rest thereon, the sanctifiers of Your name.
Blessed are You, יהוה, Who sanctifies Shabbat.

AMIDAH

On Rosh Chodesh, and on the intermediate days of festivals:

אֱלֹהֵֽינוּ וֵאלֹהֵי אֲבוֹתֵֽינוּ וְאִמּוֹתֵֽינוּ, Eloheinu veilohei avoteinu v'imoteinu,
יַעֲלֶה וְיָבֹא, וְיַגִּֽיעַ, וְיֵרָאֶה, ya·aleh v'yavo, v'yagi·a, v'yeira·eh,
וְיֵרָצֶה, וְיִשָּׁמַע, וְיִפָּקֵד, v'yeiratzeh, v'yishama, v'yipakeid,
וְיִזָּכֵר זִכְרוֹנֵֽנוּ וּפִקְדוֹנֵֽנוּ, v'yizacheir zichroneinu ufikdoneinu,
וְזִכְרוֹן אֲבוֹתֵֽינוּ וְאִמּוֹתֵֽינוּ, v'zichron avoteinu v'imoteinu,
וְזִכְרוֹן מָשִֽׁיחַ בֶּן דָּוִד עַבְדֶּֽךָ, v'zichron mashi·ach ben David avdecha,
וְזִכְרוֹן יְרוּשָׁלַֽיִם עִיר קָדְשֶֽׁךָ, vzichron Yerushalayim ir kodshecha,
וְזִכְרוֹן כָּל עַמְּךָ בֵּית יִשְׂרָאֵל לְפָנֶֽיךָ, v'zichron kol am'cha beit Yisra·el l'fanecha,
לִפְלֵיטָה, לְטוֹבָה, lifleitah, l'tovah,
לְחֵן וּלְחֶֽסֶד וּלְרַחֲמִים, l'chein ulchesed ulrachamim,
לְחַיִּים וּלְשָׁלוֹם, l'chayim ulshalom,
בְּיוֹם b'yom

לראש חדש: רֹאשׁ הַחֹֽדֶשׁ הַזֶּה. Rosh Chodesh: **Rosh haChodesh hazeh.**
לפסח: חַג הַמַּצּוֹת הַזֶּה. Pesach: Chag haMatzot hazeh.
לסכות: חַג הַסֻּכּוֹת הַזֶּה. Sukkot: Chag haSukkot hazeh.

זָכְרֵֽנוּ, יהוה, אֱלֹהֵֽינוּ, Zochreinu, יהוה, Eloheinu,
בּוֹ לְטוֹבָה, bo l'tovah,
וּפָקְדֵֽנוּ בוֹ לִבְרָכָה, ufokdeinu vo livrachah,
וְהוֹשִׁיעֵֽנוּ בוֹ לְחַיִּים, v'hoshi·einu vo l'chayim,
וּבִדְבַר יְשׁוּעָה וְרַחֲמִים, uvidvar y'shu·ah v'rachamim,
חוּס וְחָנֵּֽנוּ, chus v'choneinu,
וְרַחֵם עָלֵֽינוּ v'racheim aleinu
וְהוֹשִׁיעֵֽנוּ, v'hoshi·einu,
כִּי אֵלֶֽיךָ עֵינֵֽינוּ, ki eilecha eineinu,
כִּי אֵל מֶֽלֶךְ חַנּוּן וְרַחוּם אָֽתָּה. ki El melech chanun v'rachum atah.

On Rosh Chodesh, and on the intermediate days of festivals:

Our God and God of our ancestors:
allow memory to ascend,
to come, to reach us.
May our memory
and our ancestors' memory
and the memory of the dream
of a messianic time,
and the memory of the vision
of Jerusalem as a city of peace,
and the memories of all of Your people
of the House of Israel,
be before You

on this day of (Rosh Chodesh) (Pesach) (Sukkot).

On this day,
may these memories,
these dreams of redemption,
inspire graciousness, lovingkindness,
and compassion in us,
for life and for peace.
Remember us, יהוה, our God, for goodness.
Count us in for blessing.
Save us with life.
Shower us with salvation
and with compassion;
be merciful to us; enfold us
in the compassion we knew
before we were born.
For You are our merciful Parent and Sovereign.

מוֹדִים אֲנַחְנוּ לָךְ, שָׁאַתָּה הוּא,
יהוה אֱלֹהֵינוּ וֵאלֹהֵי
אֲבוֹתֵינוּ וְאִמּוֹתֵינוּ,
לְעוֹלָם וָעֶד, צוּרֵנוּ צוּר חַיֵּינוּ,
מָגֵן יִשְׁעֵנוּ,
אַתָּה הוּא לְדוֹר וָדוֹר,
נוֹדֶה לְּךָ וּנְסַפֵּר תְּהִלָּתֶךָ,
עַל חַיֵּינוּ הַמְּסוּרִים בְּיָדֶךָ,
וְעַל נִשְׁמוֹתֵינוּ הַפְּקוּדוֹת לָךְ,
וְעַל נִסֶּיךָ שֶׁבְּכָל יוֹם עִמָּנוּ,
וְעַל נִפְלְאוֹתֶיךָ וְטוֹבוֹתֶיךָ
שֶׁבְּכָל עֵת, עֶרֶב וָבֹקֶר וְצָהֳרָיִם:
הַטּוֹב, כִּי לֹא כָלוּ רַחֲמֶיךָ,
וְהַמְרַחֵם, כִּי לֹא תַמּוּ חֲסָדֶיךָ,
כִּי מֵעוֹלָם קִוִּינוּ לָךְ.

Modim anachnu lach, sha·atah hu,
יהוה Eloheinu veilohei
avoteinu v'imoteinu,
l'olam va·ed, tzureinu tzur chayeinu,
magein yisheinu,
atah hu l'dor vador,
nodeh l'cha unsaper t'hilatecha,
al chayeinu ham'surim b'yadecha,
v'al nishmoteinu hap'kudot lach,
v'al nisecha sheb'chol yom imanu,
v'al nifl'otecha v'tovotecha
sheb'chol eit, erev vavoker v'tzohorayim:
hatov, ki lo chalu rachamecha,
v'hamracheim, ki lo tamu chasadecha,
ki mei·olam kivinu lach.

We are grateful before You,
for You, יהוה our God and God of our ancestors, are forever
the Rock of our lives, the shield of our salvation.
You are this for us in every generation.
For our lives which are in Your hands,
and our souls which are in Your keeping,
and for the wonders You do for us each day
and the miracles You perform for us at every moment,
evening and morning and afternoon:
Your mercies never end;
Your compassion never fails;
we put our hope in You.

On Chanukah and Purim:

עַל הַנִּסִּים, וְעַל הַפֻּרְקָן,
וְעַל הַגְּבוּרוֹת, וְעַל הַתְּשׁוּעוֹת,
וְעַל הַנִּפְלָאוֹת,
שֶׁעָשִׂיתָ לַאֲבוֹתֵינוּ וּלְאִמּוֹתֵינוּ
בַּיָּמִים הָהֵם בַּזְּמַן הַזֶּה.

Al hanisim, v'al hapurkan,
v'al hag'vurot, v'al hat'shu·ot,
v'al hanifla·ot,
she·asita la·avoteinu ulimoteinu
bayamim haheim baz'man hazeh.

For the miracles, for the redemption,
for the mighty deeds, for the saving acts,
and for the wonders, which You wrought for our ancestors
in those days, at this time.

On Chanukah:

בִּימֵי מַתִּתְיָהוּ כֹּהֵן גָּדוֹל
חַשְׁמוֹנַאי וּבָנָיו כְּשֶׁעָמְדָה עֲלֵיהֶם
מַלְכוּת אַנְטְיוֹכוֹס הָרָשָׁע
וּבִקֵּשׁ לַעֲקוֹר אֶת אֱמוּנָתֵינוּ
וְדָתֵנוּ וְהֵצֵרוּ לָנוּ וְכָבְשׁוּ אֶת
הֵיכָלֵנוּ טִמְּאוּ אֶת מִקְדָּשֵׁנוּ.
אָז קָמוּ נֶגְדָּם חֲסִידֶיךָ
וְכֹהֲנֶיךָ, וְאַתָּה, בְּרַחֲמֶיךָ
הָרַבִּים, עָמַדְתָּ לָהֶם בְּעֵת צָרָתָם,
רַבְתָּ אֶת רִיבָם, נָקַמְתָּ אֶת
נִקְמָתָם, וְהָיִיתָ בְּעֶזְרָתָם לְהִתְגַּבֵּר
עֲלֵיהֶם וּלְטַהֵר אֶת הַמִּקְדָּשׁ.
מִתּוֹךְ גַּעֲגוּעִים לְהַשְׁרָאָתְךָ
רָצוּ לְהַדְלִיק אֶת הַמְּנוֹרָה
הַטְּהוֹרָה וְלֹא מָצְאוּ שֶׁמֶן
עַד שֶׁהֶרְאֵיתָ לָהֶם שֶׁמֶן טָהוֹר
לְיוֹם אֶחָד. בְּבִטָּחוֹן הִדְלִיקוּ
אֶת הַמְּנוֹרָה וְאַתָּה עָשִׂיתָ לָהֶם
נֵס וָפֶלֶא וְהַשֶּׁמֶן לֹא הִפְסִיק
עַד שֶׁעָשׂוּ מֵחָדָשׁ.
וְקָבְעוּ שְׁמוֹנַת יְמֵי חֲנֻכָּה אֵלּוּ
לְהַדְלִיק נֵרוֹת לְפִרְסוּם הַנֵּס
לְהוֹדוֹת בְּהַלֵּל לְשִׁמְךָ הַגָּדוֹל
וְהַקָּדוֹשׁ עַל נִסֶּיךָ
וְעַל נִפְלְאוֹתֶךָ וְעַל יְשׁוּעָתֶךָ.

Bimei Mattityahu kohein gadol
chashmonai uvanav k'she·amdah aleihem
malchut Antiyochos harasha
uvikeish la·akor et emunateinu
v'dateinu v'heitzeiru lanu v'chav'shu et
heichaleinu tim'u et mikdasheinu.
Az kamu negdam chasidecha
v'chohanecha, v'atah, b'rachamecha
harabim, amadta lahem b'eit tzaratam,
ravta et rivam, nakamta et
nikmatam, v'hayita b'ezratam l'hitgabeir
aleihem ultaheir et hamikdash.
Mitoch ga·agu·im l'hashra·at'cha
ratzu l'hadlik et hamenorah
hat'horah v'lo matz'u shemen
ad shehereita lahem shemen tahor
l'yom echad. B'vitachon hidliku
et hamenorah v'atah asita lahem
neis vafeleh v'hashemen lo hifsik
ad she·asu meichadash.
V'kav'u sh'monat y'mei chanukah
eilu l'hadlik neirot l'firsum haneis
l'hodot b'hallel l'shimcha hagadol
v'hakadosh al nisecha
v'al nifl'otecha v'al y'shu·atecha.

On Chanukah:

In the days of High Priest Mattityahu and his sons, when there arose against them the reign of wicked Antiochus, who sought to uproot our faith and law, oppressing us, they conquered our Temple and desecrated our sanctuary. Then there arose, against them, Your devout priests, and You, in Your great compassion, stood by them, in their troubles, waging their wars, avenging their pain, helping them to overcome Antiochus' forces and to purify the sanctuary. Amidst their longing for Your Presence among them, they sought to kindle the pure lamp and, not finding enough pure oil, You led them to find some, just enough for one day. In trust, they kindled the lamp, and You miraculously made the oil last until they could make some afresh. Then did they set these days of Chanukah to lighting candles, to chanting the Hallel, in gratitude to Your great reputation for Your miracles, Your wonders, and Your salvation.

(adaptation and translation: R' Zalman Schachter-Shalomi z"l)

On Purim:

בִּימֵי מָרְדְּכַי וְאֶסְתֵּר בְּשׁוּשַׁן הַבִּירָה, כְּשֶׁעָמַד עֲלֵיהֶם הָמָן הָרָשָׁע, בִּקֵּשׁ לְהַשְׁמִיד, לַהֲרֹג וּלְאַבֵּד אֶת כָּל הַיְהוּדִים, מִנַּעַר וְעַד זָקֵן, טַף וְנָשִׁים, בְּיוֹם אֶחָד בִּשְׁלֹשָׁה עָשָׂר לְחֹדֶשׁ שְׁנֵים עָשָׂר, הוּא חֹדֶשׁ אֲדָר, וּשְׁלָלָם לָבוֹז. וְאַתָּה בְּרַחֲמֶיךָ הָרַבִּים הֵפַרְתָּ אֶת עֲצָתוֹ, וְקִלְקַלְתָּ אֶת מַחֲשַׁבְתּוֹ, וַהֲשֵׁבוֹתָ לּוֹ גְּמוּלוֹ בְּרֹאשׁוֹ.

Bimei Mordechai v'Ester b'Shushan habirah, k'she·amad aleihem Haman harasha, bikeish l'hashmid, laharog ulabeid et kol haihudim, mina·ar v'ad zakein, taf v'nashim, b'yom echad bishlosha asar l'chodesh sh'neim asar, hu chodesh Adar, ushlalam lavoz. V'atah b'rachamecha harabim heifarta et atzato, v'kilkalta et mach·shavto, vahasheivota lo g'mulo b'rosho.

In the days of Mordechai and Esther in Shushan, the capital,
when the wicked Haman arose before them and sought to destroy,
to slay, and to exterminate all the Jews —
young and old, infants and women
— on the same day, the thirteenth of the twelfth month,
which is the month of Adar, and to plunder their possessions:
You, in Your abundant mercy, nullified his counsel and frustrated his intention
and caused his design to return upon his own head.

וְעַל כֻּלָּם יִתְבָּרַךְ וְיִתְרוֹמַם V'al kulam yitbarach v'yit·romam
שִׁמְךָ מַלְכֵּנוּ shimcha Malkeinu
תָּמִיד לְעוֹלָם וָעֶד, tamid l'olam va·ed,

For all these things, O God, let Your name forever be praised.

During the Ten Days of Repentance:
וּכְתֹב לְחַיִּים טוֹבִים כָּל בְּנֵי בְרִיתֶךָ, uchtov l'chayim tovim kol b'nei v'ritecha,
May all the children of Your covenant be inscribed for a life of goodness,

---

וְכֹל הַחַיִּים יוֹדוּךָ סֶּלָה, v'chol hachayim yoducha selah,
וִיהַלְלוּ אֶת שִׁמְךָ vihal'lu et shimcha
בֶּאֱמֶת, be·emet,
הָאֵל יְשׁוּעָתֵנוּ וְעֶזְרָתֵנוּ סֶלָה. ha·El y'shu·ateinu v'ezrateinu selah.
בָּרוּךְ אַתָּה, יהוה, Baruch atah, יהוה,
הַטּוֹב שִׁמְךָ וּלְךָ נָאֶה לְהוֹדוֹת. hatov shimcha ulcha na·eh l'hodot.

for You are the God of our redemption and our hope.
Blessed are You, יהוה, whose Name is good
and who does great things worthy of our thanksgiving.

עֹשֶׂה שָׁלוֹם בִּמְרוֹמָיו, Oseh shalom bimromav,
הוּא יַעֲשֶׂה שָׁלוֹם עָלֵינוּ Hu ya·aseh shalom aleinu
וְעַל כָּל יִשְׂרָאֵל, v'al kol Yisra·el,
וְעַל כָּל יוֹשְׁבֵי תֵבֵל, v'al kol yosh'vei teiveil,
וְאִמְרוּ: אָמֵן. v'imru: Amen.

May the One who makes peace in the heavens
make peace for us,
for all Israel,
and for all who dwell on earth.
And let us say: Amen.

Birkat Hashalom / Blessing for Peace

We cannot undo what has been done to us
nor what we have done to others
for time's arrow flies in one direction only.
So let peace come
to the rubble of history in which we stand.
Let peace come
to the hill on which the Temple used to sit.
Let peace come
to the pit from which the Twin Towers used to rise.
Let peace come
to our souls
surrounded by the ghosts of friends
of family
of lovers
and of ancestors.
Let peace come
to the ghosts of Afghans
of Koreans, North and South
of Irish, Protestant and Catholic
of Cherokee
of Romans
of Palestinians and of Israelis.
Let the rubble grow no higher.
Let peace come.

Blessed are You, Compassionate One,
who bids us gather the rubble into a foundation for peace.

(Mark Nazimova)

Elohai N'tzor

אֱלֹהַי, נְצוֹר לְשׁוֹנִי מֵרָע,	Elohai, n'tzor l'shoni meira,
וּשְׂפָתַי מִדַּבֵּר מִרְמָה,	us'fatai midabeir mirmah,
וְלִמְקַלְלַי נַפְשִׁי תִדֹּם,	v'limkal'lai nafshi tidom,
וְנַפְשִׁי כֶּעָפָר לַכֹּל תִּהְיֶה.	v'nafshi ke·afar lakol tih'yeh.
פְּתַח לִבִּי בְּתוֹרָתֶךָ,	P'tach libi b'Toratecha,
וּבְמִצְוֹתֶיךָ תִּרְדּוֹף נַפְשִׁי.	uv'mitzvotecha tirdof nafshi.
וְכָל הַחוֹשְׁבִים עָלַי רָעָה,	V'chol hachoshvim alai ra·ah,
מְהֵרָה הָפֵר עֲצָתָם	m'heirah hafeir atzatam
וְקַלְקֵל מַחֲשַׁבְתָּם.	v'kalkeil machashavtam.
עֲשֵׂה לְמַעַן שְׁמֶךָ,	Aseih l'ma·an sh'mecha,
עֲשֵׂה לְמַעַן יְמִינֶךָ,	aseih l'ma·an y'minecha,
עֲשֵׂה לְמַעַן קְדֻשָּׁתֶךָ.	aseih l'ma·an k'dushatecha,
עֲשֵׂה לְמַעַן תּוֹרָתֶךָ.	aseih l'ma·an Toratecha.
לְמַעַן יֵחָלְצוּן יְדִידֶיךָ,	L'ma·an yeichaltzun y'didecha,
הוֹשִׁיעָה יְמִינְךָ וַעֲנֵנִי.	hoshi·ah y'mincha va·aneini.

My God, guard my speech from evil and my lips from deception.
Before those who slander me, I will hold my tongue; I will practice humility.
Open my heart to Your Torah, that I may pursue Your mitzvot.
As for all who think evil of me, cancel their designs and frustrate their schemes.
Act for Your own sake, for the sake of Your Power,
for the sake of Your Holiness, for the sake of Your Torah,
so that Your loved ones may be rescued.
Save with Your power, and answer me.

יִהְיוּ לְרָצוֹן אִמְרֵי פִי	Yihihu l'ratzon imrei fi
וְהֶגְיוֹן לִבִּי	v'hegyon libi
לְפָנֶיךָ יהוה צוּרִי וְגוֹאֲלִי.	L'fanecha יהוה tzuri v'goali.

May the words of my mouth and the meditations of my heart
Be acceptable to You, יהוה, my Rock and my Redeemer.

Sanctuary

O Lord, prepare me to be a sanctuary
Pure and holy, tried and true
And in thanksgiving I'll be a living
Sanctuary for You!

וַעֲשׂוּ לִי מִקְדָּשׁ V'asu li mikdash
וְשָׁכַנְתִּי בְּתוֹכָם V'shachanti b'tocham
וַאֲנַחְנוּ נְבָרֵךְ יָהּ Va·anachnu n'varech Yah
מֵעַתָּה וְעַד עוֹלָם! Meata v'ad olam!

The Kaddish: A Door

*In all of its forms, the Kaddish is a doorway
between one part of the service and the next.*

*As we move through this door, notice:
what is happening in your heart and mind?*

*Whatever is arising in you,
bring that into your prayer.*

Chatzi Kaddish / Half Kaddish

יִתְגַּדַּל וְיִתְקַדַּשׁ שְׁמֵהּ רַבָּא.	Yitgadal v'yitkadash sh'meih raba.
בְּעָלְמָא דִּי בְרָא כִרְעוּתֵהּ,	b'alma di v'ra chiruteih,
וְיַמְלִיךְ מַלְכוּתֵהּ.	v'yamlich malchuteih
בְּחַיֵּיכוֹן וּבְיוֹמֵיכוֹן,	b'chayeichon uvyomeichon,
וּבְחַיֵּי דְכָל בֵּית יִשְׂרָאֵל,	uvchayei d'chol beit Yisra·el
בַּעֲגָלָא וּבִזְמַן קָרִיב; וְאִמְרוּ: **אָמֵן.**	ba·agala uvizman kariv; v'imru: **Amen.**
יְהֵא שְׁמֵהּ רַבָּא מְבָרַךְ	Y'hei sh'meih raba m'varach
לְעָלַם וּלְעָלְמֵי עָלְמַיָּא.	l'alam ul·almei almaya.
יִתְבָּרַךְ וְיִשְׁתַּבַּח וְיִתְפָּאַר	Yitbarach v'yishtabach v'yitpa·ar
וְיִתְרוֹמַם וְיִתְנַשֵּׂא וְיִתְהַדָּר	v'yit·romam v'yitnasei v'yit·hadar
וְיִתְעַלֶּה וְיִתְהַלָּל שְׁמֵהּ דְּקֻדְשָׁא	v'yitaleh v'yit'halal sh'meih d'kudsha
בְּרִיךְ הוּא,	**brich Hu**
לְעֵלָּא מִן כָּל בִּרְכָתָא וְשִׁירָתָא,	l'eila min kol birchata v'shirata,
תֻּשְׁבְּחָתָא וְנֶחֱמָתָא,	tushb'chata v'nechemata,
דַּאֲמִירָן בְּעָלְמָא,	da·amiran b'alma,
וְאִמְרוּ אָמֵן.	v'imru Amen.

Magnified and sanctified! Magnified and sanctified!
May God's Great Name fill the world God created.
May God's splendor be seen in the world in your life,
in your days, in the life of all Israel. Quickly and soon! And let us say, Amen.

Forever may the Great Name be blessed!

Blessed and praised! Splendid and supreme!
May the holy Name, Bless God, be praised,
far beyond all the blessings and songs,
 comforts and consolations,
that can be offered in this world.

And let us say: Amen.

(Translated by Rabbi Daniel Brenner)

Torah Service

אֵין כָּמוֹךָ בָאֱלֹהִים, יהוה, Ein kamocha va-Elohim, יהוה,
וְאֵין כְּמַעֲשֶׂיךָ. ve-ein kema·asecha.
מַלְכוּתְךָ מַלְכוּת כָּל עֹלָמִים, Malchut'cha malchut kol olamim
וּמֶמְשַׁלְתְּךָ בְּכָל דֹּר וָדֹר. umemshalt'cha b'chol dor vador.
יהוה מֶלֶךְ, יהוה מָלָךְ, יהוה melech, יהוה malach,
יהוה יִמְלֹךְ לְעֹלָם וָעֶד. יהוה yimloch l'olam va-ed.
יהוה עֹז לְעַמּוֹ יִתֵּן יהוה oz l'amo yitein,
יהוה יְבָרֵךְ אֶת עַמּוֹ בַשָּׁלוֹם. יהוה y'vareich et amo vashalom.

There is none like You among the gods, יהוה, and there are no deeds like Yours.
You are sovereign over all worlds, and Your dominion is in all generations.
יהוה reigns, יהוה has reigned, יהוה will reign forever and ever!
יהוה will give strength to our people; יהוה will bless our people with peace.

אַב הָרַחֲמִים, Av harachamim,
הֵיטִיבָה בִרְצוֹנְךָ אֶת צִיּוֹן. heitivah virtzon'cha et Tziyon.
תִּבְנֶה חוֹמוֹת יְרוּשָׁלָיִם. Tivneh chomot Yerushalayim.
כִּי בְךָ לְבַד בָּטָחְנוּ, Ki v'cha levad batachnu,
מֶלֶךְ אֵל רָם וְנִשָּׂא, אֲדוֹן עוֹלָמִים. melech El ram venisa, adon olamim.

Source of mercy: favor Zion with Your goodness; rebuild Jerusalem.
In You alone do we trust, God of space and time.

וַיְהִי בִּנְסֹעַ הָאָרֹן Vayehi binso·a ha·aron
וַיֹּאמֶר מֹשֶׁה, קוּמָה יהוה, vayomer Moshe: Kumah יהוה,
וְיָפֻצוּ אֹיְבֶיךָ, v'yafutzu oyvecha
וְיָנֻסוּ מְשַׂנְאֶיךָ מִפָּנֶיךָ. v'yanusu m'sanecha mipanecha.
כִּי מִצִּיּוֹן תֵּצֵא תוֹרָה, Ki miTzion teitzeh Torah,
וּדְבַר יהוה מִירוּשָׁלָיִם. ud'var יהוה mi'Yerushalayim.
בָּרוּךְ שֶׁנָּתַן תּוֹרָה לְעַמּוֹ יִשְׂרָאֵל Baruch shenatan Torah, l'amo Yisra·el
בִּקְדֻשָּׁתוֹ. bik'dushato.

When the Ark used to travel, Moshe would cry out:
"Rise up, יהוה, and may those who oppose us be scattered.
For Torah is coming from Zion, and the word of יהוה from Jerusalem!"
Blessed is the One Who gives Torah to us in holiness!

Repeat the next two lines after the prayer-leader:

שְׁמַע יִשְׂרָאֵל, יהוה אֱלֹהֵינוּ, Sh'ma Yisra·el, יהוה eloheinu,
יהוה אֶחָד. יהוה echad.

אֶחָד אֱלֹהֵינוּ, גָּדוֹל אֲדוֹנֵנוּ, Echad eloheinu, gadol adoneinu,
קָדוֹשׁ שְׁמוֹ. kadosh sh'mo.

גַּדְּלוּ לַיהוה אִתִּי, Gadlu la-יהוה iti,
וּנְרוֹמְמָה שְׁמוֹ יַחְדָּו. u'n'romemah sh'mo yachdav.

Hear, O Israel; יהוה is our God; יהוה is One.
One is our God, great, holy, and awesome!

Magnify God with me, and together let us elevate the Name.

לְךָ יהוה הַגְּדֻלָּה וְהַגְּבוּרָה L'cha יהוה hag'dulah v'hag'vurah
וְהַתִּפְאֶרֶת וְהַנֵּצַח וְהַהוֹד, v'hatiferet v'hanetzach v'hahod,
כִּי כֹל בַּשָּׁמַיִם וּבָאָרֶץ. ki chol bashamayim u'va·aretz.
לְךָ יהוה הַמַּמְלָכָה L'cha יהוה hamamlachah
וְהַמִּתְנַשֵּׂא לְכֹל לְרֹאשׁ. v'hamitnasei l'chol lerosh.
רוֹמְמוּ יהוה אֱלֹהֵינוּ Romemu יהוה Eloheinu,
וְהִשְׁתַּחֲווּ לַהֲדֹם רַגְלָיו vehishtachavu lahadom raglav
קָדוֹשׁ הוּא. kadosh hu,
רוֹמְמוּ יהוה אֱלֹהֵינוּ, Romemu יהוה Eloheinu,
וְהִשְׁתַּחֲווּ לְהַר קָדְשׁוֹ, vehishtachavu l'har kodsho
כִּי קָדוֹשׁ יהוה אֱלֹהֵינוּ. ki kadosh יהוה Eloheinu.

To You, יהוה, belong great lovingkindness (*chesed*),
strength (*gevurah*),
balance (*tiferet*),
endurance (*netzach*) and splendor (*hod*):
all that is on heaven and on earth.
You are sovereign, supreme above all.
Lift up your hearts to יהוה,
and bow (bend your hearts) at God's holy mountain,
because יהוה is holy!

Blessing before Torah

Traditional: highlights the uniqueness of the Jewish people

בָּרוּךְ אַתָּה יהוה Baruch atah יהוה
אֱלֹהֵינוּ מֶלֶךְ הָעוֹלָם, Eloheinu melech ha·olam,
אֲשֶׁר בָּחַר בָּנוּ מִכָּל הָעַמִּים asher bachar banu mikol ha·amim
וְנָתַן לָנוּ אֶת תּוֹרָתוֹ. v'natan lanu et Torato.
בָּרוּךְ אַתָּה יהוה, נוֹתֵן הַתּוֹרָה. Baruch atah יהוה, notein haTorah.

Holy One of Blessing, Your presence fills creation.
You have chosen us from among all the peoples to receive Your Torah.
Blessed are You, יהוה, giver of the Torah.

Alternative version: revised wording emphasizes inclusivity

בָּרוּךְ אַתָּה יהוה Baruch atah יהוה
אֱלֹהֵינוּ מֶלֶךְ הָעוֹלָם, Eloheinu melech ha·olam,
אֲשֶׁר בָּחַר בָּנוּ עִם כָּל הָעַמִּים asher bachar banu im kol ha·amim
וְנָתַן לָנוּ אֶת תּוֹרָתוֹ. v'natan lanu et Torato.
בָּרוּךְ אַתָּה יהוה, נוֹתֵן הַתּוֹרָה. Baruch atah יהוה, notein haTorah.

Holy One of Blessing, Your presence fills creation.
You have chosen us along with all peoples to receive Your Torah.
Blessed are You, יהוה, giver of the Torah.

Blessing after Torah

בָּרוּךְ אַתָּה יהוה Baruch atah, יהוה,
אֱלֹהֵינוּ מֶלֶךְ הָעוֹלָם. eloheinu melech ha·olam.
אֲשֶׁר נָתַן לָנוּ תּוֹרַת אֱמֶת, Asher natan lanu Torat emet,
וְחַיֵּי עוֹלָם נָטַע בְּתוֹכֵנוּ. v'chayyei olam nata b'tocheinu.
בָּרוּךְ אַתָּה יהוה, נוֹתֵן הַתּוֹרָה. Baruch atah, יהוה, notein hatorah!

Holy One of Blessing, Your Presence fills creation.
This Torah is a teaching of truth, and from it comes
eternal life for the people who embrace it.
Blessed are You, Merciful One, giver of the Torah!

Mi Shebeirach / Prayer for Healing

מִי שֶׁבֵּרַךְ אֲבוֹתֵינוּ,	Mi shebeirach avoteinu,
אַבְרָהָם, יִצְחָק, וְיַעֲקֹב,	Avraham, Yitzchak, v'Ya·akov,
וְאִמּוֹתֵינוּ, שָׂרָה, רִבְקָה, רָחֵל, וְלֵאָה,	v'imoteinu, Sarah, Rivkah, Rachel, v'Le·ah,
הוּא יְבָרֵךְ אֶת חוֹלֵי הַנֶּפֶשׁ,	hu y'vareich et cholei hanefesh,
חוֹלֵי הָרוּחַ, וְחוֹלֵי הַגּוּף.	cholei haru·ach, v'cholei haguf.
הַקָּדוֹשׁ בָּרוּךְ הוּא יִהְיֶה עִמָּהֶם	Hakadosh, baruch hu, yihiyeh imahem
וּשְׁמָר לָהֶם.	ush'mar lahem.
חַזֵּק אֶת־יָדָם בְּאֹמֶץ־לֵב בְּכָל יוֹם,	Chazeik et yadam b'ometz-lev b'chol yom,
בְּתוֹךְ שְׁאָר כָּל הַחוֹלִים	b'toch sha·ar kol ha·cholim
הַשְׁתָּא בַּעֲגָלָא וּבִזְמַן קָרִיב,	hashta ba·agala uvizman kariv;
וְנֹאמַר: אָמֵן.	v'nomar: Amen.

May the One who blessed our ancestors,
Abraham, Isaac and Jacob, Sarah, Rebecca, Rachel and Leah,
bless those in need of healing of body, mind, and spirit.
May the compassion of the Holy One be upon them
and watch over them.
Strengthen them with courage in each day, along with all who are ill,
now and swiftly.
And let us say: Amen.

Waters of Healing

May the waters of healing flow through our soul
May the waters of healing flow through our mind
May the waters of healing flow through our heart
May the waters of healing flow through our form.

Ana el na, please Holy One,
Refa na la, let Your healing be done
Ana el na, heal our soul,
Refa na la, may we be whole.

May the pure light of healing flow through our soul
May the pure light of healing flow through our mind
May the pure light of healing flow through our heart
May the pure light of healing flow through our form.

(Rabbi Shohama Wiener)

Broken-Hearted (HaRofei, Psalm 147)

הָרֹפֵא לִשְׁבוּרֵי לֵב Ha·ro·fei lish·vu·rei lev
וּמְחַבֵּשׁ לְעַצְּבוֹתָם. Um·cha·besh le·'atz·vo·tam.

מוֹנֶה מִסְפָּר לַכּוֹכָבִים Mo·neh mis·par la·ko·cha·vim
לְכֻלָּם שֵׁמוֹת יִקְרָא. Le·chu·lam she·mot yik·ra

Healer of the broken-hearted
Binder of their wounds
Counter of uncountable stars
You know where they are

Healer of the broken-hearted
Binder of our wounds
Counter of uncountable stars
You know who we are

הַלְלוּ יָהּ Ha·l'lu. YAH x2
אָנָּא, אֵל נָא A·na, EL na
רְפָא נָא לָהּ Re·fa na lah

אָנָּא אֵל נָא A·na EL na
רְפָא נָא לָהּ re·fa na lah x2
הַלְלוּ יָהּ Ha·l'lu. YAH x2

(Shir Yaakov Feit)

Haftarah

Blessing Before the Haftarah

בָּרוּךְ אַתָּה יהוה Baruch atah יהוה
אֱלֹהֵינוּ מֶלֶךְ הָעוֹלָם, Eloheinu melech ha·olam,
אֲשֶׁר בָּחַר בִּנְבִיאִים טוֹבִים, asher bachar bin'vi·im tovim,
וְרָצָה בְדִבְרֵיהֶם הַנֶּאֱמָרִים בָּאֱמֶת, v'ratzah v'divreiheim hane·emarim ba·emet,
בָּרוּךְ אַתָּה יהוה, baruch atah יהוה,
הַבּוֹחֵר בַּתּוֹרָה וּבְמֹשֶׁה עַבְדּוֹ, habocher baTorah u'v'Moshe avdo,
וּבְיִשְׂרָאֵל עַמּוֹ, u'v'Yisra·el amo,
וּבִנְבִיאֵי הָאֱמֶת וָצֶדֶק. uvinvi·ei ha·emet vatzedek.

Blessed are You, יהוה our God, source of all,
who has chosen good prophets and has delighted
in the faithful words they have spoken.
Blessed are You יהוה, who continues to choose
Torah, Moses, the people Israel, and prophets of truth and justice.

Blessings After the Haftarah

בָּרוּךְ אַתָּה יהוה Baruch atah יהוה
אֱלֹהֵינוּ מֶלֶךְ הָעוֹלָם, Eloheinu melech ha·olam,
צוּר כָּל הָעוֹלָמִים, tzur kol ha·olamim,
צַדִּיק בְּכָל הַדּוֹרוֹת, tzaddik b'chol ha-dorot,
הָאֵל הַנֶּאֱמָן הָאוֹמֵר וְעֹשֶׂה, ha·el hane·eman haomer v'oseh,
הַמְדַבֵּר וּמְקַיֵּם, ha'm'daber u'm'kayem,
שֶׁכָּל דְּבָרָיו אֱמֶת וָצֶדֶק. shekol d'varav emet vatzedek.

עַל הַתּוֹרָה, וְעַל הָעֲבוֹדָה, Al hatorah, v'al ha·avoda,
וְעַל הַנְּבִיאִים, וְעַל יוֹם הַשַּׁבָּת הַזֶּה v'al han'vi·im, v'al yom haShabbat hazeh
שֶׁנָּתַתָּ לָנוּ יהוה אֱלֹהֵינוּ, shenatata lanu יהוה eloheinu,
לִקְדֻשָּׁה וְלִמְנוּחָה, לְכָבוֹד וּלְתִפְאָרֶת. likdusha v'limnucha, l'chavod u'l'tifaret.

עַל הַכֹּל יהוה אֱלֹהֵינוּ, Al hakol יהוה Eloheinu,
אֲנַחְנוּ מוֹדִים לָךְ, וּמְבָרְכִים אוֹתָךְ, anachnu modim lach, u'm'varchim otach,
יִתְבָּרַךְ שִׁמְךָ בְּפִי כָּל חַי yitbarach shimcha b'fi kol chai
תָּמִיד לְעוֹלָם וָעֶד tamid l'olam va·ed
וּדְבָרְךָ אֱמֶת וְקַיָּם לָעַד. u'd'varecha emet v'kayam la·ad.
בָּרוּךְ אַתָּה יהוה, Baruch atah יהוה,
מְקַדֵּשׁ הַשַּׁבָּת וְיִשְׂרָאֵל. m'kadesh haShabbat v'Yisra·el.

Blessed are You, יהוה our God, source of all, rock of all time and space, righteous in every generation, the faithful God whose word is deed, who speaks and establishes, whose every word is truth and justice.

We thank You for the Torah and worship, for the prophets, for this Shabbat that You have given us, יהוה our God, for holiness and rest, for honor and splendor.

We thank You for everything, יהוה our God. Let Your name ever be blessed by all that lives. Your word is true forever. Blessed are You, יהוה, source of all the earth, who sanctifies Shabbat and the people Israel.

Returning the Torah to the Ark

(Woodcut by Jonathan Gibbs.)

כִּי לֶקַח טוֹב נָתַתִּי לָכֶם:	Ki lekach tov natati lachem:
תּוֹרָתִי אַל תַּעֲזֹבוּ.	Torati, al ta·azovu.
עֵץ חַיִּים הִיא לַמַּחֲזִיקִים בָּהּ,	Etz chayyim hi, lemachazikim ba
וְתֹמְכֶיהָ מְאֻשָּׁר.	V'tomche'ha m'ushar.
דְּרָכֶיהָ דַרְכֵי נֹעַם,	D'racheha darchei noam
וְכָל נְתִיבוֹתֶיהָ שָׁלוֹם.	v'chol n'tivoteha, shalom.
הֲשִׁיבֵנוּ יהוה, אֵלֶיךָ וְנָשׁוּבָה,	Hashivenu יהוה elecha v'nashuva!
חַדֵּשׁ יָמֵינוּ כְּקֶדֶם.	Chadesh yameinu k'kedem!

I have given you my Torah: do not forsake it.
It is a tree of life to those who hold it fast.
All its paths are paths of pleasantness, and its ways are ways of peace.
Turn us, O God, and we will return to You!
Renew, renew our days as of old!

Chatzi Kaddish / Half Kaddish

יִתְגַּדַּל וְיִתְקַדַּשׁ שְׁמֵהּ רַבָּא.	Yitgadal v'yitkadash sh'meih raba.
בְּעָלְמָא דִּי בְרָא כִרְעוּתֵהּ,	b'alma di v'ra chiruteih,
וְיַמְלִיךְ מַלְכוּתֵהּ.	v'yamlich malchuteih
בְּחַיֵּיכוֹן וּבְיוֹמֵיכוֹן	b'chayeichon uvyomeichon,
וּבְחַיֵּי דְכָל בֵּית יִשְׂרָאֵל,	uvchayei d'chol beit Yisra·el
בַּעֲגָלָא וּבִזְמַן קָרִיב וְאִמְרוּ: **אָמֵן.**	ba·agala uvizman kariv; v'imru: **Amen.**
יְהֵא שְׁמֵהּ רַבָּא מְבָרַךְ	Y'hei sh'meih raba m'varach
לְעָלַם וּלְעָלְמֵי עָלְמַיָּא.	l'alam ul·almei almaya.
יִתְבָּרַךְ וְיִשְׁתַּבַּח וְיִתְפָּאַר	Yitbarach v'yishtabach v'yitpa·ar
וְיִתְרוֹמַם וְיִתְנַשֵּׂא וְיִתְהַדָּר	v'yit·romam v'yitnasei v'yit·hadar
וְיִתְעַלֶּה וְיִתְהַלָּל שְׁמֵהּ דְּקֻדְשָׁא	v'yitaleh v'yit'halal sh'meih d'kudsha
בְּרִיךְ הוּא,	**brich Hu**
לְעֵלָּא מִן כָּל בִּרְכָתָא וְשִׁירָתָא,	l'eila min kol birchata v'shirata,
תֻּשְׁבְּחָתָא וְנֶחֱמָתָא,	tushb'chata v'nechemata,
דַּאֲמִירָן בְּעָלְמָא,	da·amiran b'alma,
וְאִמְרוּ אָמֵן.	v'imru Amen.

Magnified and sanctified! Magnified and sanctified!
May God's Great Name fill the world God created.
May God's splendor be seen in the world in your life,
in your days, in the life of all Israel. Quickly and soon! And let us say, Amen.

Forever may the Great Name be blessed!

Blessed and praised! Splendid and supreme!
May the holy Name, Bless God, be praised,
far beyond all the blessings and songs,
comforts and consolations,
that can be offered in this world.

And let us say: Amen.

(Translated by Rabbi Daniel Brenner)

Musaf: "Extra"

Musaf means "additional," and refers to the additional service we offer on Shabbat and festivals, a reminder of the additional offerings we once made at the Temple in Jerusalem on holy days.

(Photograph by Ze'ev Barkan)

In Place of A Formal Amidah

Questions for Silent Contemplation

What is the additional prayer you want to add this morning?

What is the prayer you haven't yet prayed, the offering of your heart that you still need to give over?

Enter your heart even more deeply. What is waiting there to be silently expressed?

Kedushat HaYom: The Holiness of This Day (for Shabbat Musaf)

Six days each week are holy days,
their spans established by darkening skies.

But every seventh day brings in *gad* and *mazal*,
this sacrosanct day fixed by one setting sun and three glittering stars.
Mark this day.
Bless its Creator.
Set aside this seventh day for exaltation.

Those who seek delight will taste worlds within its boundaries;
since before Sinai,
those who love it and hold it close are choosers of life,
eternally.

Absorb its Torah, its offerings and its laws without ceasing.
And make one additional offering
to the One who presents this day to us.

(Rabbi Janet Madden)

Kedushah Keter: The Crown

Keter:
the highest heaven,
the innermost chamber.

The heart, still
as the calmest waters,
basks in Your light.

In this place (that is not a place)
we mirror the angels on high.
All we can say is

Holy, holy, holy
Holy, holy, holy
Holy, holy, holy!

Let our words be Your crown.
Let Your radiance
shine through us.

(Rabbi Rachel Barenblat)

Yismechu: Rejoice

יִשְׂמְחוּ בְמַלְכוּתְךָ Yism'chu v'malchut'cha
שׁוֹמְרֵי שַׁבָּת וְקוֹרְאֵי עֹנֶג, shomrei Shabbat v'korei oneg.
עַם מְקַדְּשֵׁי שְׁבִיעִי, Am m'kad'shei shvi·i,
כֻּלָּם יִשְׂבְּעוּ וְיִתְעַנְּגוּ מִטּוּבֶךָ, kulam yisb'u v'yitangu mituvecha,
וּבַשְּׁבִיעִי רָצִיתָ בּוֹ וְקִדַּשְׁתּוֹ, ubashvi·i ratzita bo v'kidashto,
חֶמְדַּת יָמִים אוֹתוֹ קָרָאתָ, chemdat yamim oto karata,
זֵכֶר לְמַעֲשֵׂה בְרֵאשִׁית. zecher l'ma·aseh v'reishit.

Those who keep Shabbat by calling it a delight will rejoice in You.
The people that hallow Shabbat will delight in Your goodness.
For, being pleased with the seventh day, You made it holy
as the most precious of days, reminding us of the work of Creation.

Offering: What We Do For Love

we take the blow for another,
or we keep quiet about the blows we're dealt,
give too much of what we have
because it is exactly the shape of another's need.
we fling our lives aside to rush to a bedside, a shiva, an airport,
a distant highway's shoulder,
switch seats, sit through, stay behind, sally forth,
let them stand in our sun or shade.
we keep their secrets, or let them keep their illusions
or risk their rage when we don't.
we give up the umbrella,
keep watch, ignore the score, wait around,
resist giving in to what is small and mean within us.
sometimes we lie. sometimes we don't.
we leave the sacrifice on the altar
and, on the table, the last slice of cake
we give and give up
and hope that it is enough, and then,
somehow,
begin again.

(Jacqui Shine)

Tikanta Shabbat: You Instituted Shabbat...

In ancient days when we visited the temple, additional sacrifices made way for additional songs and additional prayers and additional opportunities to come close to God. We watched our words ascend to the heavens lifted up from the altar by smoke. We had few things but lots of time so we offered what was precious to us to give substance to our prayers.

Today with calculators and clocks and metrics, hourly wages and billing hours, time has become more precious than things. Every minute counts and lost time is lost money and it takes time to come close to God. We listen to our prayers fly away to the heavens guided by the ticking of our watches and the beating of our hearts. We have lots of things but little time so we offer what is precious to us to give substance to our prayers.

Smoke rises up and time flies away. Neither can return. May our prayers today be joined to our prayers of old as we return to God.

(Rabbi Lewis John Eron)

Descending Through the Alphabet

A reverse alphabetic acrostic from ת to א

אדוני	Adonai	*My God, open* my lips in prayer...
תפתח	tiftach	
תפארת	Tiferet	that I might praise your *glory*.
שירים	Shirim	I sing *songs* of joy and thanks
רחמים	Rachamim	enveloped in your *compassionate* embrace.
קדוש	Kadosh	*Holy, holy, holy,*
צור	Tsur	my *rock* and my redeemer.
פנים	Panim	Your *Presence* is with me always
ערב	Erev	Morning, noon, and *evening*.
סלה	Selah	*Selah!*
נשמה	Neshama	My *spirit* soars,
מודים	Modim	tears of *gratitude* spill from my eyes,
לב	Lev	my *heart* is full.
כבוד	Kavod	I bend and bow in your *honor*.
יהי רצון	Y'hi Ratzon	*May it be your will* that I may serve you all my days.
טוב	Tov	Your *goodness* and grace have touched me, uplifted me,
חסד	Chesed	your *lovingkindness* soothes my soul.

ורופא	V'rofeh	Dear God, I pray: *Heal* me when I am in pain.
הולך	Holech	when I *walk* upon the road, when I lie down and when I rise up.
דרך	Derech	Show me your *way* when I am alone, and comfort me
גאלי	Go'ali	My rock and my *redeemer*,
ברוך	Baruch	*bless* me and keep me,
אמהות/ אבות	Imahot / Avot	by the merit of my *mothers* and my *fathers*, this I pray.

(Rabbi Jennifer Singer)

Psalm 29: Chant

יהוה עֹז לְעַמּוֹ יִתֵּן, יהוה oz l'amo yitein,
יהוה יְבָרֵךְ אֶת עַמּוֹ בַשָּׁלוֹם. יהוה y'varech et amo vashalom.

May יהוה grant strength to God's people;
may יהוה bestow wholeness on God's people.

Psalm 29: Full-text

מִזְמוֹר לְדָוִד, הָבוּ לַיהוה	Mizmor leDavid, havu la'יהוה
בְּנֵי אֵלִים, הָבוּ לַיהוה כָּבוֹד וָעֹז.	b'nei eilim, havu la'יהוה kavod va·oz.
הָבוּ לַיהוה כְּבוֹד שְׁמוֹ,	Havu la'יהוה k'vod sh'mo,
הִשְׁתַּחֲווּ לַיהוה בְּהַדְרַת קֹדֶשׁ.	hishtachavu la'יהוה b'hadrat kodesh.
קוֹל יהוה עַל הַמָּיִם,	Kol יהוה al hamayim,
אֵל הַכָּבוֹד הִרְעִים,	El hakavod hirim,
יהוה עַל מַיִם רַבִּים.	יהוה al mayim rabim.
קוֹל יהוה בַּכֹּחַ, קוֹל יהוה בֶּהָדָר.	Kol יהוה bako·ach, kol יהוה behadar.
קוֹל יהוה שֹׁבֵר אֲרָזִים,	Kol יהוה shoveir arazim,
וַיְשַׁבֵּר יהוה אֶת אַרְזֵי הַלְּבָנוֹן.	vay'shabeir יהוה et arzei hal'vanon.
וַיַּרְקִידֵם כְּמוֹ עֵגֶל,	Va'yarkideim k'mo eigel,
לְבָנוֹן וְשִׂרְיוֹן כְּמוֹ בֶן רְאֵמִים.	l'vanon v'siryon k'mo ven r'eimim.
קוֹל יהוה חֹצֵב לַהֲבוֹת אֵשׁ.	Kol יהוה chotzeiv lahavot eish.
קוֹל יהוה יָחִיל מִדְבָּר,	Kol יהוה yachil midbar,
יָחִיל יהוה מִדְבַּר קָדֵשׁ.	yachil יהוה Midbar Kadesh.
קוֹל יהוה יְחוֹלֵל אַיָּלוֹת,	Kol יהוה y'choleil ayalot,
וַיֶּחֱשֹׂף יְעָרוֹת, וּבְהֵיכָלוֹ,	vayechesof y'arot, u'vheikhalo,
כֻּלּוֹ אֹמֵר כָּבוֹד.	kulo omeir kavod.
יהוה לַמַּבּוּל יָשָׁב,	יהוה lamabul yashav,
וַיֵּשֶׁב יהוה מֶלֶךְ לְעוֹלָם.	va'yeishev יהוה melech l'olam.
יהוה עֹז לְעַמּוֹ יִתֵּן,	יהוה oz l'amo yitein,
יהוה יְבָרֵךְ אֶת עַמּוֹ בַשָּׁלוֹם.	יהוה y'vareich et amo vashalom.

A psalm of David. Ascribe to יהוה, O divine beings,
ascribe to יהוה glory and strength.
Ascribe to יהוה the glory of God's name; bow down to יהוה, majestic in holiness.
The voice of יהוה is over the waters;
the God of glory thunders, יהוה, over the mighty waters.
The voice of יהוה is power; the voice of יהוה is majesty;
the voice of יהוה breaks cedars; יהוה shatters the cedars of Lebanon.
God makes Lebanon skip like a calf, Sirion, like a young wild ox.
The voice of יהוה kindles flames of fire; the voice of יהוה convulses the wilderness;
יהוה convulses the wilderness of Kadesh; the voice of יהוה causes hinds to calve,
and strips forests bare; while in God's temple all say "Glory!"
יהוה sat enthroned at the Flood; יהוה sits enthroned, king forever.
May יהוה grant strength to God's people;
may יהוה bestow wholeness on God's people.

Chatzi Kaddish / Half Kaddish

יִתְגַּדַּל וְיִתְקַדַּשׁ שְׁמֵהּ רַבָּא. Yitgadal v'yitkadash sh'meih raba.
בְּעָלְמָא דִּי בְרָא כִרְעוּתֵהּ, b'alma di v'ra chiruteih,
וְיַמְלִיךְ מַלְכוּתֵהּ. v'yamlich malchuteih
בְּחַיֵּיכוֹן וּבְיוֹמֵיכוֹן, b'chayeichon uvyomeichon,
וּבְחַיֵּי דְכָל בֵּית יִשְׂרָאֵל, uvchayei d'chol beit Yisra·el
בַּעֲגָלָא וּבִזְמַן קָרִיב; וְאִמְרוּ: **אָמֵן.** ba·agala uvizman kariv; v'imru: **Amen.**

יְהֵא שְׁמֵהּ רַבָּא מְבָרַךְ Y'hei sh'meih raba m'varach
לְעָלַם וּלְעָלְמֵי עָלְמַיָּא. l'alam ul·almei almaya.

יִתְבָּרַךְ וְיִשְׁתַּבַּח וְיִתְפָּאַר Yitbarach v'yishtabach v'yitpa·ar
וְיִתְרוֹמַם וְיִתְנַשֵּׂא וְיִתְהַדָּר v'yit·romam v'yitnasei v'yit·hadar
וְיִתְעַלֶּה וְיִתְהַלָּל שְׁמֵהּ דְּקֻדְשָׁא v'yitaleh v'yit'halal sh'meih d'kudsha
בְּרִיךְ הוּא, **brich Hu**
לְעֵלָּא מִן כָּל בִּרְכָתָא וְשִׁירָתָא l'eila min kol birchata v'shirata,
תֻּשְׁבְּחָתָא וְנֶחֱמָתָא, tushb'chata v'nechemata,
דַּאֲמִירָן בְּעָלְמָא, da·amiran b'alma,
וְאִמְרוּ אָמֵן. v'imru Amen.

Magnified and sanctified! Magnified and sanctified!
May God's Great Name fill the world God created.
May God's splendor be seen in the world in your life,
in your days, in the life of all Israel. Quickly and soon! And let us say, Amen.

Forever may the Great Name be blessed!

Blessed and praised! Splendid and supreme!
May the holy Name, Bless God, be praised,
far beyond all the blessings and songs,
comforts and consolations,
that can be offered in this world.

And let us say: Amen.

(Translated by Rabbi Daniel Brenner)

Ein k'Eloheinu

אֵין כֵּאלֹהֵינוּ, אֵין כַּאדוֹנֵנוּ, Ein k'Eloheinu, ein k'adoneinu,
אֵין כְּמַלְכֵּנוּ, אֵין כְּמוֹשִׁיעֵנוּ. Ein k'malkeinu, ein k'moshienu.

מִי כֵאלֹהֵינוּ, מִי כַאדוֹנֵנוּ, Mi ch'Eloheinu, mi ch'adoneinu,
מִי כְמַלְכֵּנוּ, מִי כְמוֹשִׁיעֵנוּ. Mi ch'malkeinu, mi ch'moshienu.

נוֹדֶה לֵאלֹהֵינוּ, נוֹדֶה לַאדוֹנֵנוּ, Nodeh le-Eloheinu, nodeh l'adoneinu,
נוֹדֶה לְמַלְכֵּנוּ, נוֹדֶה לְמוֹשִׁיעֵנוּ. Nodeh l'malkeinu, nodeh l'moshienu.

בָּרוּךְ אֱלֹהֵינוּ, בָּרוּךְ אֲדוֹנֵנוּ, Baruch Eloheinu, baruch adoneinu,
בָּרוּךְ מַלְכֵּנוּ, בָּרוּךְ מוֹשִׁיעֵנוּ. Baruch malkeinu baruch moshienu.

אַתָּה הוּא אֱלֹהֵינוּ, אַתָּה הוּא אֲדוֹנֵנוּ, Atah hu Eloheinu, atah hu adoneinu,
אַתָּה הוּא מַלְכֵּנוּ, אַתָּה הוּא מוֹשִׁיעֵנוּ. Atah hu malkeinu, atah hu moshienu.

אַתָּה הוּא שֶׁהִקְטִירוּ אֲבוֹתֵינוּ Atah hu she'hiktiru avoteinu
לְפָנֶיךָ אֶת קְטֹרֶת הַסַּמִּים. L'fanecha et k'toret hasamim.

There is none like our God, there is none like our Lord,
There is none like our King, there is none like our Salvation.

Who is like our God? Who is like our Lord?
Who is like our King? Who is like our Salvation?

Let us thank our God! Let us thank our Lord!
Let us thank our King! Let us thank our Salvation!

Blessed be our God, blessed be our Lord,
Blessed be our King, blessed be our Salvation!

You alone are our God; You alone are our Lord,
You alone are our King, You alone are our Salvation.

You are the one to Whom our ancestors burned incense,
Coming before you with sweet spices.

Non komo muestro Dyo

This is "Ein k'Eloheinu" in Ladino, also known as Judeo-Spanish.

נון קומו מואישטרו דיו,	Non komo muestro Dyo,
נון קומו מואישטרו שינייור,	Non komo muestro Senyor,
נון קומו מואישטרו ריאי,	Non komo muestro Rey,
נון קומו מואישטרו שלבַּדור.	Non komo muestro Salvador.
קיין קומו מואישטרו דיו,	Kien komo muestro Dyo,
קיין קומו מואישטרו שינייור,	Kien komo muestro Senyor,
קיין קומו מואישטרו ריאי,	Kien komo muestro Rey,
קיין קומו מואישטרו שלבַּדור.	Kien komo muestro Salvador.
לוארימוס אה מואישטרו דיו,	Loaremos a muestro Dyo,
לוארימוס אה מואישטרו שינייור,	Loaremos a muestro Senyor,
לוארימוס אה מואישטרו ריאי,	Loaremos a muestro Rey,
לוארימוס אה מואישטרו שלבַּדור.	Loaremos a muestro Salvador.
בנדיגו מואישטרו דיו,	Bendicho muestro Dyo,
בנדיגו מואישטרו שינייור,	Bendicho muestro Senyor,
בנדיגו מואישטרו ריאי,	Bendicho muestro Rey,
בנדיגו מואישטרו שלבַּדור.	Bendicho muestro Salvador.
טו סוס מואישטרו דיו,	Tu sos muestro Dyo,
טו סוס מואישטרו שינייור,	Tu sos muestro Senyor.
טו סוס מואישטרו ריאי,	Tu sos muestro Rey,
טו סוס מואישטרו שלבַּדור.	Tu sos muestro Salvador.

(Morning Service) Closings

Aleinu

Aleinu Chants

Ein Od Milvado

אֵין עוֹד מִלְבַדּוֹ, Ein od milvado;
יהוה הוּא הָאֱלֹהִים. יהוה hu ha·Elohim.

There is nothing but God.

V'hasheivota (Call and Response)

וַהֲשֵׁבֹתָ Vahasheivota
אֶל לְבָבֶךָ El levavecha
כִּי יהוה Ki יהוה
הוּא הָאֱלֹהִים Hu ha·Elohim.

(Return to your heart:
know that God Who is Infinite is also God Who is close to us.)

וְנֶאֱמַר, V'ne·emar,
וְהָיָה יהוה לְמֶלֶךְ עַל כָּל הָאָרֶץ, יהוה v'haya lemelech al kol ha·aretz,
בַּיּוֹם הַהוּא יִהְיֶה יהוה אֶחָד, bayom hahu yihyeh יהוה echad
וּשְׁמוֹ אֶחָד. ushmo echad.

(And it is said: on that day יהוה will be God over all the earth,
and on that day יהוה will be One and God's Name will be One.)

Full Text Aleinu

עָלֵינוּ לְשַׁבֵּחַ לַאֲדוֹן הַכֹּל, Aleinu l'shabei·ach la·adon hakol,
לָתֵת גְּדֻלָּה לְיוֹצֵר בְּרֵאשִׁית, lateit g'dulah l'yotzeir b'reishit.
שֶׁלֹּא/שֶׁלּוֹ* Shelo
עָשָׂנוּ כְּגוֹיֵי הָאֲרָצוֹת, asanu k'goyei ha·aratzot,
וְלֹא/וְלוֹ* v'lo
שָׂמָנוּ כְּמִשְׁפְּחוֹת הָאֲדָמָה. samanu k'mishp'chot ha·adamah.
שֶׁלֹּא/שֶׁלּוֹ* Shelo
שָׂם חֶלְקֵנוּ כָּהֶם, sam chelkeinu kahem,
וְגוֹרָלֵנוּ כְּכָל הֲמוֹנָם. v'goraleinu k'chol hamonam.

It is up to us to praise the Source of all, to exalt the Molder of creation. We are:
      made for God   (or)   not made like
      like all nations.   other nations.

We are:
      placed here for God (or)   unlike
      like all humanity.   other peoples.

Our portion and our fate are:
      for God's   (or)   not like those
      own sake.   of other peoples.

וַאֲנַחְנוּ כּוֹרְעִים Va·anachnu korim,
וּמִשְׁתַּחֲוִים וּמוֹדִים, umishtachavim umodim,
לִפְנֵי מֶלֶךְ, מַלְכֵי הַמְּלָכִים, lifnei melech malchei ham'lachim,
הַקָּדוֹשׁ בָּרוּךְ הוּא. hakadosh baruch hu.

We bow low and prostrate in thanks
before the Source of all sources, the Holy One, blessed is God.

---

*Pray either לֹא, pronounced lo ("not"), or לוֹ, also pronounced lo ("for God"). The first articulates Jewish chosenness; the second, post-triumphalism.

(MORNING SERVICE) CLOSINGS

שֶׁהוּא נוֹטֶה שָׁמַיִם וְיֹסֵד אָרֶץ,   Shehu noteh shamayim v'yoseid aretz,
וּמוֹשַׁב יְקָרוֹ בַּשָּׁמַיִם מִמַּעַל,   umoshav y'karo bashamayim mima·al,
וּשְׁכִינַת עֻזּוֹ בְּגָבְהֵי מְרוֹמִים.   ush·chinat uzo b'govhei m'romim.
הוּא אֱלֹהֵינוּ אֵין עוֹד.   Hu Eloheinu, ein od.

אֱמֶת מַלְכֵּנוּ אֶפֶס זוּלָתוֹ,   Emet malkeinu efes zulato.
כַּכָּתוּב בְּתוֹרָתוֹ:   Kakatuv b'Torato:
וְיָדַעְתָּ הַיּוֹם וַהֲשֵׁבֹתָ אֶל לְבָבֶךָ,   "V'yadata hayom vahasheivota el l'vavecha,
כִּי יהוה הוּא הָאֱלֹהִים   ki יהוה hu ha·Elohim
בַּשָּׁמַיִם מִמַּעַל,   bashamayim mima·al,
וְעַל הָאָרֶץ מִתַּחַת, אֵין עוֹד.   v'al ha·aretz mitachat, ein od."

God sets out the heavens and establishes the earth.
God's honored place is in the heights of our aspirations;
God's powerful presence is in the heavens of our hopes.
This is our God, there is none else. There is nothing that God is not.

עַל כֵּן נְקַוֶּה לְךָ יהוה אֱלֹהֵינוּ,   Al kein nekaveh lecha יהוה Eloheinu,
לִרְאוֹת מְהֵרָה בְּתִפְאֶרֶת עֻזֶּךָ,   lirot m'heirah b'tiferet uzecha,
לְהַעֲבִיר גִּלּוּלִים מִן הָאָרֶץ   l'ha·avir gilulim min ha·aretz
וְהָאֱלִילִים כָּרוֹת יִכָּרֵתוּן.   veha·elilim karot yikareitun
לְתַקֵּן עוֹלָם בְּמַלְכוּת שַׁדַּי,   l'takein olam bemalchut Shadai.
וְכָל בְּנֵי בָשָׂר יִקְרְאוּ בִשְׁמֶךָ.   V'chol b'nei vasar yikr'u vishmecha·
לְהַפְנוֹת אֵלֶיךָ כָּל רִשְׁעֵי אָרֶץ.   L'hafnot eilecha kol rishei aretz.
יַכִּירוּ וְיֵדְעוּ כָּל יוֹשְׁבֵי תֵבֵל,   Yakiru veyeidu kol yoshvei teiveil
כִּי לְךָ תִּכְרַע כָּל בֶּרֶךְ   ki l'cha tichra kol berech
תִּשָּׁבַע כָּל לָשׁוֹן.   tishava kol lashon.

Therefore we hope in You, יהוה our God,
to see soon the power of Your beauty wipe away false gods from the earth
and sweep away idolatry,
so that the truth of Your sovereign presence will repair the world.
Then will all humanity call Your name
and then all that had been dark will turn to Your light.
All who dwell on earth will feel in their hearts and know in their minds
that You are our source—the true object of devotion and loyalty.

לְפָנֶיךָ יהוה אֱלֹהֵינוּ יִכְרְעוּ וְיִפֹּלוּ. L'fanecha יהוה Eloheinu yichr'u v'yipolu
וְלִכְבוֹד שִׁמְךָ יְקָר יִתֵּנוּ. v'lichvod shimcha y'kar yiteinu.
וִיקַבְּלוּ כֻלָּם אֶת עֹל מַלְכוּתֶךָ. Vikablu chulam et ol malchutech,
וְתִמְלֹךְ עֲלֵיהֶם מְהֵרָה לְעוֹלָם וָעֶד. v'timloch aleihem m'heirah l'olam va·ed.
כִּי הַמַּלְכוּת שֶׁלְּךָ הִיא, Ki hamalchut shelcha hi,
וּלְעוֹלְמֵי עַד תִּמְלוֹךְ בְּכָבוֹד. ul'olmei ad timloch b'chavod.

Before You, יהוה our God, will they bend low and pay homage
to glorify Your name.
Then all will accept the obligations of living in Your world—
obligations of hope, love and duty to heaven and humanity.
Then You will surely rule forever and ever.
For the earth is Yours and Your glory fills it forever.

כַּכָּתוּב בְּתוֹרָתֶךָ, Kakatuv b'Toratecha,
יהוה יִמְלֹךְ לְעֹלָם וָעֶד. יהוה yimloch l'olam va·ed.
וְנֶאֱמַר, וְהָיָה יהוה לְמֶלֶךְ V'ne·emar, v'haya יהוה lemelech
עַל כָּל הָאָרֶץ, al kol ha·aretz.
בַּיּוֹם הַהוּא יִהְיֶה יהוה אֶחָד, Bayom hahu yihyeh יהוה echad,
וּשְׁמוֹ אֶחָד. ush'mo echad!

As it is written in God's sacred teaching:
"You shall know this day and place upon your heart
that יהוה is God in heaven above and earth below;
there is none else."

Then shall your realm be established on earth,
and the word of Your prophet fulfilled:
"יהוה will reign forever and ever.
On that day, יהוה shall be One, and God's name shall be One."

There is no other

| עָלֵינוּ | Aleinu | It is upon us |

It is upon us to repair the broken places.
It is upon us to comfort the sick in body and heart.
It is upon us to bring joy to those around us.

It is upon us to face the truth, no matter how difficult.
It is upon us to see that justice is is done, which is not always easy.
It is upon us to know when we have choices, and to make them.

It is upon us to understand that our prayers are holy conversations.
It is upon us to be mindful and to notice what we see with compassion.
It is upon us to aspire to God's presence.

| וַאֲנַחְנוּ כֹּרְעִים | Va·anachnu kor'im | We bend knee and bow… |

We bend our knees to acknowledge
how small we are in the face of all this responsibility.
We bend our knees to warm up for all the hard work.
We bend our knees to dance.

| אֵין עוֹד | Ein od | There is no other |

We are all one in the One-ness, there is no other.
Amen.

(Trisha Arlin)

Mourner's *Kaddish*

יִתְגַּדַּל וְיִתְקַדַּשׁ שְׁמֵהּ רַבָּא. Yitgadal v'yitkadash, sh'meih raba (Amen)
בְּעָלְמָא דִּי בְרָא כִרְעוּתֵהּ, B'alma di v'ra chiruteih, v'yamlich
וְיַמְלִיךְ מַלְכוּתֵהּ malchuteih

[In communities that follow nusach sefarad:
(וְיַצְמַח פֻּרְקָנֵהּ וִיקָרֵב מְשִׁיחֵהּ) *vikareiv m'shicheih v'yatzmach purkaneih]*

בְּחַיֵּיכוֹן וּבְיוֹמֵיכוֹן b'chayeichon uv'yomeichon
וּבְחַיֵּי דְכָל בֵּית יִשְׂרָאֵל. uvchayei d'chol beit Yisra·el.
בַּעֲגָלָא וּבִזְמַן קָרִיב וְאִמְרוּ אָמֵן. Ba·agala uvizman kariv v'imru **Amen**.

יְהֵא שְׁמֵהּ רַבָּא מְבָרַךְ **Y'hei sh'mei raba m'varakh**
לְעָלַם וּלְעָלְמֵי עָלְמַיָּא. **l'olam ol'almey almaya.**

יִתְבָּרַךְ וְיִשְׁתַּבַּח, Yitbarach v'yishtabach,
וְיִתְפָּאַר וְיִתְרוֹמַם וְיִתְנַשֵּׂא. v'yitpa·ar v'yit-romam v'yitnaseh.
וְיִתְהַדָּר וְיִתְעַלֶּה V'yit·hadar v'yitaleh
וְיִתְהַלָּל שְׁמֵהּ דְּקֻדְשָׁא **בְּרִיךְ הוּא** v'yit-hallal sh'meihd'kud·h'sha **b'rich hu**.
לְעֵלָּא מִן כָּל בִּרְכָתָא וְשִׁירָתָא, L'eyla min kol birchata v'shirata,
תֻּשְׁבְּחָתָא וְנֶחֱמָתָא, tushbechata v'nechemata,
דַּאֲמִירָן בְּעָלְמָא, וְאִמְרוּ אָמֵן. damiran b'alma, v'imru amen.

יְהֵא שְׁלָמָא רַבָּא מִן שְׁמַיָּא Y'hei shlama raba min shemaya
וְחַיִּים עָלֵינוּ וְעַל כָּל יִשְׂרָאֵל, v'chayim aleinu v'al kol Yisra·el,
וְאִמְרוּ אָמֵן. v'imru amen.
עֹשֶׂה שָׁלוֹם בִּמְרוֹמָיו Oseh shalom bimromav,
הוּא יַעֲשֶׂה שָׁלוֹם hu ya·aseh shalom,
עָלֵינוּ וְעַל כָּל יִשְׂרָאֵל, aleinu v'al kol Yisra·el,
וְעַל כָּל יוֹשְׁבֵי תֵבֵל, וְאִמְרוּ אָמֵן. v'al kol yoshvei teiveil, v'imru: **Amen**.

The Great Essence will flower in our lives
And expand throughout the world.
May we learn to let it shine through so we can augment its glory.
We praise, we continue to praise,
And yet, whatever it is we praise, is quite beyond the grasp
Of all the words and symbols that point us toward it.
We know, yet we do not know.
May great peace pour forth from the heavens for us,
For all Israel, and for all who struggle toward truth.
May that which makes harmony in the cosmos above,
Bring peace within and between us, and to all who dwell on this earth.
May the Source of peace send peace to all who mourn
And comfort all who are bereaved.

(Translation: Rabbi Burt Jacobson)

Songs

Yigdal

This hymn is based on Maimonides' 13 Articles of Faith; this version was written by Daniel ben Judah Dayan, and was completed in 1404.

יִגְדַּל אֱלֹהִים חַי וְיִשְׁתַּבַּח,   Yigdal Elohim chai v'yishtabach
נִמְצָא, וְאֵין עֵת אֶל מְצִיאוּתוֹ.   nimtsah ve·ein eit el metzi·uto
אֶחָד וְאֵין יָחִיד כְּיִחוּדוֹ,   Echad ve·ein yachid k'yichudo
נֶעְלָם וְגַם אֵין סוֹף לְאַחְדּוּתוֹ.   ne·elam v'gam ein sof l'achduto.

Exalt the living God, who is unbounded by time.
God is One—unique, unknowable and endless.

אֵין לוֹ דְמוּת הַגּוּף וְאֵינוֹ גוּף,   Ein lo damut haguf v'eino guf,
לֹא נַעֲרוֹךְ אֵלָיו קְדֻשָּׁתוֹ.   lo na·aroch eilav k'dushato.
קַדְמוֹן לְכָל דָּבָר אֲשֶׁר נִבְרָא,   Kadmon l'chol davar asher nivra
רִאשׁוֹן וְאֵין רֵאשִׁית לְרֵאשִׁיתוֹ.   rishon ve·ein reishit l'reishito.

God has no body or form, only holiness beyond measure.
God existed uniquely before a single thing was created.

הִנּוֹ אֲדוֹן עוֹלָם, לְכָל נוֹצָר,   Hino adon olam l'chol notzar,
יוֹרֶה גְדֻלָּתוֹ וּמַלְכוּתוֹ.   yoreh g'dulato umalchuto.
שֶׁפַע נְבוּאָתוֹ נְתָנוֹ   Shefa n'vu·ato n'tano
אֶל אַנְשֵׁי סְגֻלָּתוֹ וְתִפְאַרְתּוֹ.   el anshei s'gulato v'tifarto.

Behold, the universe is God's, and everything in it.
God's wisdom flows to those who seek God's splendor.

לֹא קָם בְּיִשְׂרָאֵל כְּמֹשֶׁה עוֹד,   Lo kam b'Yisra·el k'Moshe od,
נָבִיא וּמַבִּיט אֶת תְּמוּנָתוֹ.   navi umabit et t'munato.
תּוֹרַת אֱמֶת נָתַן לְעַמּוֹ אֵל,   Torat emet natan l'amo El,
עַל יַד נְבִיאוֹ נֶאֱמַן בֵּיתוֹ.   al yad nevi·o ne·eman beito.

No prophet like Moses shall ever come again,
Through him God gave us the Torah of truth.

(MORNING SERVICE) CLOSINGS

לֹא יַחֲלִיף הָאֵל וְלֹא יָמִיר דָּתוֹ. Lo yachalif ha·eil v'lo yamir dato,
לְעוֹלָמִים, לְזוּלָתוֹ. le·olamim l'zulato.
צוֹפֶה וְיוֹדֵעַ סְתָרֵינוּ, Tzofeh v'yodei·a s'tareinu,
מַבִּיט לְסוֹף דָּבָר בְּקַדְמָתוֹ. mabit l'sof davar b'kadmato.

God's truth is eternal and God's law is irreplaceable.
God knows our hidden places and sees from beginning to end.

גּוֹמֵל לְאִישׁ חֶסֶד כְּמִפְעָלוֹ, Gomeil l'ish chesed k'mifalo,
נוֹתֵן לְרָשָׁע רָע כְּרִשְׁעָתוֹ. notein l'rasha ra k'rishato.
יִשְׁלַח לְקֵץ הַיָּמִין מְשִׁיחֵנוּ, Yishlach lekeitz hayamin m'shicheinu,
לִפְדּוֹת מְחַכֵּי קֵץ יְשׁוּעָתוֹ. lifdot mechakei keitz y'shu·ato.

God accords good and bad according to our deeds,
God will send redemption to all who yearn to be redeemed.

מֵתִים יְחַיֶּה אֵל Meitim y'chayeh El
בְּרוֹב חַסְדּוֹ, b'rov chasdo.
בָּרוּךְ עֲדֵי עַד Baruch adei ad
שֵׁם תְּהִלָּתוֹ! sheim t'hilato!

With love, God gives life which transcends death.
Blessed is God's name, God be blessed for all eternity.

Adon Olam

אֲדוֹן עוֹלָם אֲשֶׁר מָלַךְ,	Adon olam asher malach,
בְּטֶרֶם כָּל יְצִיר נִבְרָא.	b'terem kol yetsir nivra.
לְעֵת נַעֲשָׂה בְחֶפְצוֹ כֹּל,	L'eit na·asah v'cheftso kol,
אֲזַי מֶלֶךְ שְׁמוֹ נִקְרָא.	azai melech shemo nikra.

You are the source of all, who reigned before any being was created;
When all was done according to Your will, Your rule already had been proclaimed.

וְאַחֲרֵי כִּכְלוֹת הַכֹּל,	Ve·acharei kichlot hakol,
לְבַדּוֹ יִמְלוֹךְ נוֹרָא.	levado yimloch nora.
וְהוּא הָיָה, וְהוּא הֹוֶה,	V'hu haya v'hu hoveh,
וְהוּא יִהְיֶה, בְּתִפְאָרָה.	v'hu yih'yeh b'tifarah.

And after all has ended, still, You alone will rule in majesty;
You were, You are, You will be in glory.

וְהוּא אֶחָד וְאֵין שֵׁנִי,	V'hu echad v'ein sheini,
לְהַמְשִׁיל לוֹ לְהַחְבִּירָה:	l'hamshil lo l'hachbirah.
בְּלִי רֵאשִׁית בְּלִי תַכְלִית,	B'li reishit b'li tachlit,
וְלוֹ הָעֹז וְהַמִּשְׂרָה.	v'lo ha·oz v'hamisrah.

You are One, there is none to compare or consort with You.
Without beginning, without end, all power and all order come from You.

וְהוּא אֵלִי וְחַי גֹּאֲלִי,	V'hu eili v'chai go·ali,
וְצוּר חֶבְלִי בְּעֵת צָרָה.	v'tsur chevli b'eit tzarah.
וְהוּא נִסִּי וּמָנוֹס לִי	V'hu nisi umanos li
מְנָת כּוֹסִי בְּיוֹם אֶקְרָא.	m'nat kosi b'yom ekra.

You are my God, my living redeemer, You are my rock in time of distress;
You are my banner and my refuge, You fill my cup when I cry to You.

בְּיָדוֹ אַפְקִיד רוּחִי,	B'yado afkid ruchi,
בְּעֵת אִישַׁן וְאָעִירָה.	b'eit ishan v'a·ira
וְעִם רוּחִי גְּוִיָּתִי,	V'im ruchi g'viyati,
יְהוָה לִי וְלֹא אִירָא.	Adonai li v'lo ira.

Into Your hands I entrust my spirit, When I sleep and when I wake;
And with my spirit, my body, too: You are with me, I shall not fear.

(MORNING SERVICE) CLOSINGS

from **Adon Olam: A Mystical Interpretation**

You know Adon Olam
And you know
Its simple translation:

Master of the World
Who Ruled
Before every thing
was created

But Ibn Gabirol
poet and philosopher
was not thinking simple
He was thinking deep

Adon
From biblical Hebrew:
Adanim, joints
The Matrix that holds
a structure together

Olam
Eternal in time
Infinite in space
Elusive
Hidden

Adon Olam:
The Hidden Matrix that
holds reality together

Asher
Not just a preposition
But an adjective
Happy, joyous, blissful

Adon Olam Asher
If you grasp this matrix,
you feel joy and bliss
your most sublime
moments of peace
radiate

Malach
From the word malchut,
royalty
In Kabbalah a synonym
for Shechinah
The indwelling presence
Dwelling every where

Adon Olam
Asher Malach
The indwelling elusive
matrix of bliss

B'terem
Before
in the before
in the great before

Before **Kol Yetzir**
Everything that has form
Nivra
was created
B'terem kol yetzir nivra
Before anything with
physical shape,
Anything with form
or boundaries

was created

Before even a thought
of creation,
Before a design
or a plan
arose

The indwelling
elusive matrix of bliss
existed

But "existed" is a verb
in the past tense form
And until beings
with form were created
There was no "before"
Only an indwelling
elusive
matrix of bliss
There was no infinity
Because infinite
means "not finite"
And without finite beings
Who can measure
infinity?
Infinity!

A marvelous angel,
God's first
created concept
Infinity:
a measure,
a hint,
The footsteps of time

Marked out
by the poet,
In his rhythmic words

When I
Pray
I often ask:

Holy One,
help me
hold it all,
thoughts & feelings
fears & failures
Because you,
Holy One,
already hold them

in your elusive matrix
B'yado afkid ruchi
Into this cosmic hand
I assign my spirit
Trusting it is held
in the matrix

B'et Ishan
When it's time for sleep
I, whose bodily life
is timed
By hormones, neurons,
and nutrients
Conforming to a
circadian rhythm

I surrender my control
for 8 hours
I let
the matrix
hold me

V'aiyra
Until I wake up

And beyond

V'im ruchi geviyati
With my soul expressed
through this time-bound
form

Adonai Li
My concept
of an infinite God
keeps me company

V'lo Irah
Irah, to see,
Irah, to fear

Though I will never see
the matrix
itself
It holds me
I will not fear

Rabbi Laura Duhan
Kaplan

Home

home is where my heart is beating
home is where my feet touch the ground
home is moments with a loved one
communicating without sound

home is silence, dancing, deep breath
home is where the tears are found
home is laughter, light and darkness
spilling forth and circling round

home is where i find myself
home is passion so profound
home is twilight ebbing, flowing
homeward here, homeward bound...

(Kohenet Taya Shere)
Listen to audio at https://holytaya.bandcamp.com/track/home

Chants from Psalm 27

Achat Sha·alti — Psalm 27:4

אַחַת שָׁאַלְתִּי מֵאֵת־יהוה	Achat sha·alti me·eit	One thing I ask,
אוֹתָהּ אֲבַקֵּשׁ. יהוה	otah avakesh	I ask of You: One thing do I seek
שִׁבְתִּי בְּבֵית־יהוה,	Shivti b'veit יהוה,	That I might dwell in Your house
כָּל־יְמֵי חַיַּי	kol y'mei chayyay	all the days of my life
לַחֲזוֹת בְּנֹעַם־יהוה,	Lachazot b'noam יהוה,	Knowing the beauty of You,
וּלְבַקֵּר בְּהֵיכָלוֹ.	u'levaker b'heikhalo.	and to dwell in Your holy place!

Lach Amar Libi — Psalm 27:8

לָךְ	Lach	You
אָמַר לִבִּי	amar libi	Called to my heart:
בַּקְּשׁוּ פָנָי	bakshu fanai	Come seek My face,
בַּקְּשׁוּ פָנָי.	bakshu fanai.	Come seek My grace.
אֶת פָּנֶיךָ	Et panayich	For Your love
הויה	Havayah	Source of all
אֲבַקֵּשׁ.	Avakeish.	I will seek.

Kavei el יהוה — Psalm 27:14

קַוֵּה קַוֵּה	Kavei kavei,	Keep hope, keep hope
קַוֵּה אֶל־יהוה	Kavei el יהוה.	Keep hoping in the One
חֲזַק וְיַאֲמֵץ	Chazak v'ya·ametz	Be strong and open
לִבֶּךָ	Libecha	Your heart wide
וְקַוֵּה אֶל־יהוה.	V'kavei el יהוה!	And keep hoping in the One!

Mincha: Afternoon Offering

The Sunset Prayer / Davvenen Minhah

I'll let you in on a secret
about how one should pray the sunset prayer.
It's a juicy bit of praying,
like strolling on grass,
nobody's chasing you, nobody hurries you.
You walk toward your creator
with gifts in pure, empty hands.
The words are golden,
their meaning is transparent,
it's as though you're saying them for the first time.

If you don't catch on
that you should feel a little elevated,
you're not praying the sunset prayer.
The tune is sheer simplicity,
you're just lending a helping hand
to the sinking day.
It's a heavy responsibility.
You take a created day
and you slip it
into the archive of life
where all our lived-out days are lying together.

The day is departing with a quiet kiss.
It lies open at your feet
while you stand saying the blessings.
You can't create anything yourself,
but you can lead the day to its end
and see clearly the smile of its going down.

See how whole it is,
not diminished for a second,
how you age with the days
that keep dawning,
how you bring your lived-out day
as a gift to eternity.

Jacob Glatstein
(translated from the Yiddish by Ruth Whitman)

Ashrei

There's a full-text version of the Ashrei, and a singable English rendition as well, in the Shabbat morning section of this book on p. 16.

אַשְׁרֵי יוֹשְׁבֵי בֵיתֶךָ, עוֹד יְהַלְלוּךָ סֶּלָה.
Ashrei yosh'vei veitecha. Od y'hal'lucha selah.
Happy are they who dwell in Your house; they will praise You forever.

Uva L'Tzion: A Prayer for Redemption

This prayer, part of traditional daily prayer and sung to a special melody on Shabbat afternoon, depicts angels calling out reminders of God's glory. It asks God to direct our hearts toward holiness, and reminds us that God is merciful; it expresses our hope that we may live to see messianic time when the work of creation will be complete. The translation here interprets freely.

וּבָא לְצִיּוֹן גּוֹאֵל,	U'va l'tziyon go·eil,
וּלְשָׁבֵי פֶשַׁע בְּיַעֲקֹב, נְאֻם יהוה.	u'lshavei pesha b'Ya·akov, n'um יהוה.
וַאֲנִי זֹאת בְּרִיתִי אֹתָם אָמַר יהוה,	Va·ani zot briti otam amar יהוה,
רוּחִי אֲשֶׁר עָלֶיךָ,	ruchi asher alekha,
וּדְבָרַי אֲשֶׁר שַׂמְתִּי בְּפִיךָ	u'dvarai asher samti b'fikha
לֹא יָמוּשׁוּ מִפִּיךָ, וּמִפִּי זַרְעֲךָ,	lo yamushu mipikha, u'mipi zar·akha,
וּמִפִּי זֶרַע זַרְעֲךָ, אָמַר יהוה,	u'mipi zera zar·akha, amar יהוה,
מֵעַתָּה וְעַד עוֹלָם.	mei·ata v'ad olam.

'Redemption will come to those who make *t'shuvah*,' says יהוה.
'And this is My covenant with them:
My spirit that is upon you, My words which I have given you,
will not leave you or your children, now or ever.'

אַתָּה קָדוֹשׁ,	Atah kadosh,
יוֹשֵׁב תְּהִלּוֹת יִשְׂרָאֵל.	yosheiv t'hilot Yisra·el:
וְקָרָא זֶה אֶל זֶה וְאָמַר,	v'kara zeh el zeh v'amar:
קָדוֹשׁ קָדוֹשׁ קָדוֹשׁ	**kadosh kadosh kadosh**
יהוה צְבָאוֹת,	**יהוה Tz'va·ot,**
מְלֹא כָל הָאָרֶץ כְּבוֹדוֹ.	**m'lo khol ha·aretz k'vodo.**
וּמְקַבְּלִין דֵּין מִן דֵּין, וְאָמְרִין,	U'mkab'lin dein min dein, v'am'rin,
קַדִּישׁ בִּשְׁמֵי מְרוֹמָא עִלָּאָה	Kaddish bishmei m'roma i·la·ah
בֵּית שְׁכִינְתֵּהּ,	beit sh'khintei,
קַדִּישׁ עַל אַרְעָא עוֹבַד גְּבוּרְתֵּהּ,	Kaddish al ar·a ovad g'vur·tei·h,
קַדִּישׁ לְעָלַם וּלְעָלְמֵי עָלְמַיָּא,	Kaddish l'alam u'l'al'mei almaya,
יהוה צְבָאוֹת	יהוה Tz'va·ot,
מַלְיָא כָל אַרְעָא זִיו יְקָרֵהּ.	malya khol ar·a ziv y'karei·h.
וַתִּשָּׂאֵנִי רוּחַ,	va'tisa·eini ruach,
וָאֶשְׁמַע אַחֲרַי קוֹל רַעַשׁ גָּדוֹל,	va·eshma acharai kol ra·ash gadol,
בָּרוּךְ כְּבוֹד יהוה מִמְּקוֹמוֹ.	**baruch k'vod יהוה mimkomo.**
וּנְטָלַתְנִי רוּחָא,	U'ntalatni rucha,
וְשִׁמְעֵת בַּתְרַי קָל זִיעַ סַגִּיא,	v'shimeit batrai kal zi·a sagi,
דִּמְשַׁבְּחִין וְאָמְרִין,	dimshab'chin v'am'rin,
בְּרִיךְ יְקָרָא דַיהוה	b'rich y'kara da'יהוה
מֵאֲתַר בֵּית שְׁכִינְתֵּהּ.	mei·atar beit sh'khintei:
יהוה יִמְלֹךְ לְעֹלָם וָעֶד.	**יהוה yimlokh l'olam va·ed.**
יהוה לְמַעַן יְזַמֶּרְךָ כָבוֹד וְלֹא יִדֹּם,	יהוה l'ma·an y'zamerkha kavod v'lo yidom,
יהוה אֱלֹהַי לְעוֹלָם אוֹדֶךָּ.	יהוה Elohai l'olam odeka.
בָּרוּךְ הַגֶּבֶר אֲשֶׁר יִבְטַח בַּיהוה,	Baruch hagever asher yivtach ba'יהוה,
וְהָיָה יהוה מִבְטַחוֹ.	v'haya יהוה mivtacho.
בִּטְחוּ בַיהוה עֲדֵי עַד,	Bitchu ba' יהוה adei ad,
כִּי בְּיָהּ יהוה צוּר עוֹלָמִים.	ki b'Yah יהוה tzur olamim.
וְיִבְטְחוּ בְךָ יוֹדְעֵי שְׁמֶךָ,	V'yivt'chu v'kha yod'ei sh'mekha,
כִּי לֹא עָזַבְתָּ דֹּרְשֶׁיךָ יהוה.	ki lo azavta dor'shekha יהוה.
יהוה חָפֵץ לְמַעַן צִדְקוֹ,	יהוה chafeitz l'ma·an tzidko,
יַגְדִּיל תּוֹרָה וְיַאְדִּיר.	yagdil Torah v'yadir.

You, O God, are holy, enthroned on our prayers;
and we are like the fire-angels on high,
singing one to another,
Holy, Holy, Holy is יהוה *of hosts.*
God's Presence fills the world!

We grant one another permission to pray;
we remind ourselves that God's holiness exists
both here and in the highest heavens.

We remember the vision of Ezekiel:

"A spiritwind carried me away
and I heard behind me the sound of a great roaring which said,
Blessed is the Presence of Adonai from wherever it shall be,
accompanied by the beating of vast angels' wings,
the sound of a great roaring."

Together we ask:

Help us to pray like the angels
in whose hearts and minds
holiness ricochets
like a laser beam.

Open our hearts to You, God
and to Your Torah
so that our souls might sing to You
and not be stilled.

Turn our hearts toward holiness
stir us to create healing
open our eyes to Your presence
everywhere, everywhere.

(Rabbi Rachel Barenblat)

Chatzi Kaddish

יִתְגַּדַּל וְיִתְקַדַּשׁ שְׁמֵהּ רַבָּא. Yitgadal v'yitkadash sh'meih raba. (Amen)
בְּעָלְמָא דִּי בְרָא כִרְעוּתֵהּ, b'alma di v'ra chiruteih.
וְיַמְלִיךְ מַלְכוּתֵהּ. V'yamlich malchuteih
בְּחַיֵּיכוֹן וּבְיוֹמֵיכוֹן, b'chayeichon uvyomeichon,
וּבְחַיֵּי דְכָל בֵּית יִשְׂרָאֵל, uvchayei d'chol beit Yisra-el
בַּעֲגָלָא וּבִזְמַן קָרִיב וְאִמְרוּ אָמֵן. ba·agala uvizman kariv; v'imru: Amen.

□ יְהֵא שְׁמֵהּ רַבָּא מְבָרַךְ □ Y'hei sh'meih raba m'varach
לְעָלַם וּלְעָלְמֵי עָלְמַיָּא. l'alam ul·almei almaya.

יִתְבָּרַךְ וְיִשְׁתַּבַּח וְיִתְפָּאַר Yitbarach v'yishtabach v'yitpa·ar
וְיִתְרוֹמַם וְיִתְנַשֵּׂא וְיִתְהַדָּר v'yit·romam v'yitnasei v'yit·hadar
וְיִתְעַלֶּה וְיִתְהַלָּל v'yitaleh v'yit'halal
שְׁמֵהּ דְּקֻדְשָׁא בְּרִיךְ הוּא, sh'meih d'kudsha - brich hu -
לְעֵלָּא מִן כָּל בִּרְכָתָא וְשִׁירָתָא, l'eila min kol birchata v'shirata,
תֻּשְׁבְּחָתָא וְנֶחֱמָתָא, tushb'chata v'nechemata,
דַּאֲמִירָן בְּעָלְמָא, וְאִמְרוּ אָמֵן. da·amiran b'alma; v'imru: Amen.

Magnified and sanctified! Magnified and sanctified!
May God's Great Name fill the world God created.
May God's splendor be seen in the world in your life, in your days,
in the life of all Israel.
Quickly and soon! And let us say, Amen.

Forever may the Great Name be blessed!

Blessed and praised! Splendid and supreme!
May the holy Name, Bless God, be praised,
far beyond all the blessings and songs,
comforts and consolations,
that can be offered in this world.
And let us say: Amen.

Torah

וַיְהִי בִּנְסֹעַ הָאָרֹן	Vayehi binso·a ha·aron
וַיֹּאמֶר מֹשֶׁה, קוּמָה יהוה,	vayomer Moshe: Kumah יהוה,
וְיָפֻצוּ אֹיְבֶיךָ,	v'yafutzu oyvecha,
וְיָנֻסוּ מְשַׂנְאֶיךָ מִפָּנֶיךָ.	v'yanusu m'sanecha mipanecha.
כִּי מִצִּיּוֹן תֵּצֵא תוֹרָה,	Ki miTzion teitzeh Torah,
וּדְבַר יהוה מִירוּשָׁלָיִם.	ud'var יהוה mi'Yerushalayim.
בָּרוּךְ שֶׁנָּתַן תּוֹרָה, לְעַמּוֹ יִשְׂרָאֵל	Baruch shenatan Torah, l'amo Yisra·el
בִּקְדֻשָּׁתוֹ.	bik'dushato.

When the Ark used to travel, Moshe would cry out:
"Rise up, יהוה, and may those who oppose us be scattered.
For Torah is coming from Zion, and the word of יהוה from Jerusalem!"
Blessed is the One Who gives Torah to us in holiness!

גַּדְּלוּ לַיהוה אִתִּי,	Gadlu la-יהוה iti,
וּנְרוֹמְמָה שְׁמוֹ יַחְדָּו.	u'n'romemah sh'mo yachdav.

לְךָ יהוה הַגְּדֻלָּה וְהַגְּבוּרָה	L'cha יהוה hag'dulah v'hag'vurah
וְהַתִּפְאֶרֶת וְהַנֵּצַח וְהַהוֹד,	v'hatiferet v'hanetzach v'hahod,
כִּי כֹל בַּשָּׁמַיִם וּבָאָרֶץ.	ki chol bashamayim u'va·aretz.
לְךָ יהוה הַמַּמְלָכָה	L'cha יהוה hamamlachah
וְהַמִּתְנַשֵּׂא לְכֹל לְרֹאשׁ.	v'hamitnasei l'chol lerosh.
רוֹמְמוּ יהוה אֱלֹהֵינוּ	Romemu יהוה Eloheinu,
וְהִשְׁתַּחֲווּ לַהֲדֹם רַגְלָיו	vehishtachavu lahadom raglav
קָדוֹשׁ הוּא.	kadosh hu.
רוֹמְמוּ יהוה אֱלֹהֵינוּ,	Romemu יהוה Eloheinu,
וְהִשְׁתַּחֲווּ לְהַר קָדְשׁוֹ,	vehishtachavu lahadom kodsho
כִּי קָדוֹשׁ יהוה אֱלֹהֵינוּ.	ki kadosh יהוה Eloheinu.

To You, יהוה, belong great lovingkindness (*chesed*),
strength (*gevurah*),
balance (*tiferet*),
endurance (*netzach*) and splendor (*hod*):
all that is on heaven and on earth.
You are sovereign, supreme above all.
Lift up your hearts to יהוה,
and bow (bend your hearts) at God's holy mountain,
because יהוה is holy!

MINCHA: AFTERNOON OFFERING 112

Blessing before Torah

Traditional: highlights the uniqueness of the Jewish people

בָּרוּךְ אַתָּה יהוה Baruch atah יהוה
אֱלֹהֵינוּ מֶלֶךְ הָעוֹלָם, Eloheinu melech ha·olam,
אֲשֶׁר בָּחַר בָּנוּ מִכָּל הָעַמִּים asher bachar banu mikol ha·amim
וְנָתַן לָנוּ אֶת תּוֹרָתוֹ. v'natan lanu et Torato.
בָּרוּךְ אַתָּה יהוה, נוֹתֵן הַתּוֹרָה. Baruch atah יהוה, notein hatorah.

Holy One of Blessing, Your presence fills creation.
You have chosen us from among all the peoples to receive Your Torah.
Blessed are You, יהוה, giver of the Torah.

Alternative version: revised wording emphasizes inclusivity

בָּרוּךְ אַתָּה יהוה Baruch atah יהוה
אֱלֹהֵינוּ מֶלֶךְ הָעוֹלָם, Eloheinu melech ha·olam,
אֲשֶׁר בָּחַר בָּנוּ עִם כָּל הָעַמִּים asher bachar banu im kol ha·amim
וְנָתַן לָנוּ אֶת תּוֹרָתוֹ. v'natan lanu et Torato.
בָּרוּךְ אַתָּה יהוה, נוֹתֵן הַתּוֹרָה. Baruch atah יהוה, notein hatorah.

Holy One of Blessing, Your presence fills creation.
You have chosen us along with all peoples to receive Your Torah.
Blessed are You, יהוה, giver of the Torah.

Blessing after Torah

בָּרוּךְ אַתָּה יהוה Baruch atah, יהוה,
אֱלֹהֵינוּ מֶלֶךְ הָעוֹלָם, Eloheinu melech ha·olam,
אֲשֶׁר נָתַן לָנוּ תּוֹרַת אֱמֶת, asher natan lanu Torat emet,
וְחַיֵּי עוֹלָם נָטַע בְּתוֹכֵנוּ. v'chayyei olam nata b'tocheinu.
בָּרוּךְ אַתָּה יהוה, נוֹתֵן הַתּוֹרָה. Baruch atah, יהוה, notein hatorah!

Holy One of Blessing, Your Presence fills creation.
This Torah is a teaching of truth,
and from it comes eternal life for the people who embrace it.
Blessed are You, Merciful One, giver of the Torah!

Prayers for healing can be found in the morning service on p. 78.
Liturgy for returning the Torah to the ark can be found in the morning service on p. 82.
Chatzi Kadish can be found on p. 110

Shabbat Afternoon *Amidah*

I Stand (Avot v' Imahot)

I stand on the shoulders of family
of friends, of teachers, of strangers
who themselves stand on the shoulders
of people who stood on shoulders…

each generation of shoulders
a rung on Jacob's ladder
reaching me up toward
Heaven
just beyond my grasp

(Mark Nazimova)

The full text of the Shabbat amidah can be found in the morning service on p. 55.

Contemplative *Amidah*

Imahot v'Avot / Ancestors

I reflect on my ancestors. Who did I come from? How did they shape me?

Baruch atah יהוה, magein Avraham v'ezrat Sarah.
בָּרוּךְ אַתָּה יהוה, מָגֵן אַבְרָהָם וְעֶזְרַת שָׂרָה.

Gevurot / Power

What is the source of power in my life?
Where do I find strength? What enlivens me?

Baruch atah יהוה, m'chayei hameitim.
בָּרוּךְ אַתָּה יהוה, מְחַיֵּה הַמֵּתִים.

Kedushah / Holiness

I open myself to holiness. I seek to live wholly and in a way that is holy.

Baruch atah יהוה, ha·El hakadosh.
בָּרוּךְ אַתָּה יהוה, הָאֵל הַקָּדוֹשׁ.

Shabbat

May I open myself to the gifts of this Shabbat.
As I rest, may I partake in holiness, and may my rest be a gift.
Baruch atah יהוה, m'kadesh haShabbat.
בָּרוּךְ אַתָּה יהוה, מְקַדֵּשׁ הַשַּׁבָּת.

Avoda / Service

May my life be an expression of my desire to serve something greater than myself.
May my service help to uplift Shechinah, Divine presence, everywhere.
Baruch atah יהוה, hamachazir shechinato l'tziyon.
בָּרוּךְ אַתָּה יהוה, הַמַּחֲזִיר שְׁכִינָתוֹ לְצִיּוֹן.

Hoda·a / Gratitude

Help me to cultivate gratitude for the blessings of every day.
Baruch atah יהוה, hatov shimcha u'l'cha naeh l'hodot.
בָּרוּךְ אַתָּה יהוה, הַטּוֹב שִׁמְךָ וּלְךָ נָאֶה לְהוֹדוֹת.

Shalom / Peace

Help me to feel and to embody peace and wholeness.
Baruch atah יהוה, hamvorech et amo Yisra·el bashalom.
בָּרוּךְ אַתָּה יהוה, הַמְבָרֵךְ אֶת עַמּוֹ יִשְׂרָאֵל בַּשָּׁלוֹם.

עֹשֶׂה שָׁלוֹם בִּמְרוֹמָיו	Oseh shalom bimromav,
הוּא יַעֲשֶׂה שָׁלוֹם עָלֵינוּ	hu ya·aseh shalom aleinu
וְעַל כָּל יִשְׂרָאֵל,	v'al kol Yisra·el,
וְעַל כָּל יוֹשְׁבֵי תֵבֵל,	v'al kol yoshvei teiveil,
וְאִמְרוּ אָמֵן.	v'imru Amen.

May the One who makes peace in the heavens
make peace for us, for all Israel, and for all who dwell on earth.
And let us say: Amen.

Maariv / Evening Prayer

Barchu — Call to Prayer

As we bless the Source of Life, so we are blessed.
And the blessing gives us strength, and makes our visions clear;
And the blessing gives us peace, and the courage to dare.
As we bless the Source of Life, so we are blessed.

(Faith Rogow)

V'Hu Rachum / The Merciful One

וְהוּא רַחוּם יְכַפֵּר עָוֹן וְלֹא יַשְׁחִית, V'Hu rachum y'chapeir avon v'lo yash·chit,
וְהִרְבָּה לְהָשִׁיב אַפּוֹ, v'hirbah l'hashiv apo,
וְלֹא יָעִיר כָּל חֲמָתוֹ. v'lo ya·ir kol chamato.
יהוה הוֹשִׁיעָה, יהוה hoshiya,
הַמֶּלֶךְ יַעֲנֵנוּ בְיוֹם קָרְאֵנוּ. hamelech ya·aneinu b'yom koreinu.

The Merciful One will cover iniquity and not forever destroy.
Soon may God withdraw anger; may divine rage not be aroused.
יהוה, save us, You who answer on the day when we call.

בָּרְכוּ אֶת יהוה הַמְבֹרָךְ. Bar'chu et יהוה hamvorach.

בָּרוּךְ יהוה הַמְבֹרָךְ לְעוֹלָם וָעֶד. Baruch יהוה hamvorach l'olam va·ed.

Blessed is יהוה, the blessed One.

Blessed is יהוה, the blessed One, now and forever!

Maariv Aravim: Who Evens the Evenings

בָּרוּךְ אַתָּה יהוה,	Baruch atah יהוה,
אֱלֹהֵינוּ מֶלֶךְ הָעוֹלָם,	Eloheinu, Melech ha-olam,
אֲשֶׁר בִּדְבָרוֹ מַעֲרִיב עֲרָבִים,	asher bidvaro ma·ariv aravim,
בְּחָכְמָה פּוֹתֵחַ שְׁעָרִים,	b'chochmah potei·ach sh'arim,
וּבִתְבוּנָה מְשַׁנֶּה עִתִּים,	uvitvunah m'shaneh itim,
וּמַחֲלִיף אֶת הַזְּמַנִּים,	umachalif et hazmanim,
וּמְסַדֵּר אֶת הַכּוֹכָבִים	umsadeir et hakochavim
בְּמִשְׁמְרוֹתֵיהֶם בָּרָקִיעַ כִּרְצוֹנוֹ.	b'mishm'roteihem baraki·a kirtzono.

Blessed are You, יהוה our God, Source of all being,
by Whose word the evening falls.
In wisdom You open heaven's gates.
With understanding You make seasons change,
causing the times to come and go,
and ordering the stars on their appointed paths
through heaven's dome, all according to Your will.

בּוֹרֵא יוֹם וָלָיְלָה,	Borei yom valailah,
גּוֹלֵל אוֹר מִפְּנֵי חֹשֶׁךְ,	goleil or mipnei choshech
וְחֹשֶׁךְ מִפְּנֵי אוֹר.	v'choshech mipnei or.
וּמַעֲבִיר יוֹם וּמֵבִיא לָיְלָה,	Uma·avir yom umeivi lailah,
וּמַבְדִּיל בֵּין יוֹם וּבֵין לָיְלָה,	umavdil bein yom uvein lailah,
יהוה צְבָאוֹת שְׁמוֹ.	יהוה Tz'vaot sh'mo.
אֵל חַי וְקַיָּם,	El chai v'kayam,
תָּמִיד יִמְלוֹךְ עָלֵינוּ לְעוֹלָם וָעֶד.	tamid yimloch aleinu l'olam va·ed.
בָּרוּךְ אַתָּה יהוה,	Baruch atah יהוה,
הַמַּעֲרִיב עֲרָבִים.	hama·ariv aravim.

Creator of day and night, who rolls back light before dark,
and dark before light, who makes day pass away
and brings on the night, dividing between day and night;
the Leader of Heaven's Multitudes is Your name!
Living and enduring God, be our guide now and always.
Blessed are You, Source of All being, Who makes evening fall.

MAARIV / EVENING PRAYER

Evening

You mix the watercolors of the evening
like my son, swishing his brush
until the waters are black with paint.
The sky is streaked and dimming.

The sun wheels over the horizon
like a glowing penny falling into its slot.
Day is spent, and in its place: the changing moon,
the spatterdash of stars across the sky's expanse.

Every evening we tell ourselves the old story:
You cover over our sins, forgiveness
like a fleece blanket tucked around our ears.
When we cry out, You will hear.

Soothe my fear of life without enough light.
Rock me to sleep in the deepening dark.

(Rabbi Rachel Barenblat)

Ahavat Olam: Unending Love

אַהֲבַת עוֹלָם Ahavat olam
בֵּית יִשְׂרָאֵל עַמְּךָ אָהָבְתָּ, beit Yisra·el amcha ahavta
תּוֹרָה וּמִצְוֹת, חֻקִּים וּמִשְׁפָּטִים Torah umitzvot chukim umishpatim
אוֹתָנוּ לִמַּדְתָּ. עַל כֵּן יהוה אֱלֹהֵינוּ, otanu limad'ta. Al kein יהוה Eloheinu
בְּשָׁכְבֵנוּ וּבְקוּמֵנוּ נָשִׂיחַ בְּחֻקֶּיךָ, b'shochveinu uvkumeinu nasi·ach b'chukecha.
וְנִשְׂמַח בְּדִבְרֵי תַלְמוּד תּוֹרָתֶךָ, V'nismach b'divrei talmud Toratecha,
וּבְמִצְוֹתֶיךָ לְעוֹלָם וָעֶד. uv'mitzvotecha l'olam va·ed.
כִּי הֵם חַיֵּינוּ וְאֹרֶךְ יָמֵינוּ, Ki heim chayeinu v'orech yameinu
וּבָהֶם נֶהְגֶּה יוֹמָם וָלָיְלָה. uvahem negeh yomam valailah.

וְאַהֲבָתְךָ אַל תָּסִיר מִמֶּנּוּ V'ahavat'cha al tasir mimenu
לְעוֹלָמִים. l'olamim.
בָּרוּךְ אַתָּה יהוה, Baruch atah יהוה
אוֹהֵב עַמּוֹ יִשְׂרָאֵל. oheiv amo Yisra·el.

With eternal love, You love the house of Israel.
Torah and mitzvot, laws and justice You have taught us.
And so, יהוה, our God, when we lie down and when we rise,
we reflect upon Your laws;
we take pleasure in Your Torah's words and your mitzvot, now and always.
Truly, they are our life, our length of days. On them we meditate by day and night.

Your love will never depart from us as long as worlds endure.
Blessed are You, יהוה, who loves Your people Israel.

Unending Love

We are loved by unending love.

We are embraced by arms that find us
even when we are hidden from ourselves.
We are touched by fingers that soothe us
even when we are too proud for soothing.
We are counseled by voices that guide us
even when we are too embittered to hear.

We are loved by unending love.

We are supported by hands that uplift us
even in the midst of a fall.
We are urged on by eyes that meet us
even when we are too weak for meeting.

We are loved by unending love.

Embraced, touched, soothed, and counseled,
ours are the arms, the fingers, the voices;
ours are the hands, the eyes, the smiles;

We are loved by unending love.

(Rabbi Rami Shapiro)

Sh'ma: Oneness

שְׁמַע יִשְׂרָאֵל, **Sh'ma Yisra·el:**
יהוה אֱלֹהֵינוּ, יהוה אֶחָד. יהוה **Eloheinu** יהוה **echad!**

בָּרוּךְ שֵׁם כְּבוֹד מַלְכוּתוֹ (Baruch shem k'vod malchuto
לְעוֹלָם וָעֶד. l'olam va·ed.)

Hear, O Israel: יהוה is our God, יהוה is One!
(Through time and space Your glory shines, Majestic One!)

וְאָהַבְתָּ אֵת יהוה אֱלֹהֶיךָ, V'ahavta et יהוה Elohecha,
בְּכָל לְבָבְךָ, וּבְכָל נַפְשְׁךָ, b'chol levavcha, uvchol nafsh'cha,
וּבְכָל מְאֹדֶךָ. uvchol m'odecha.
וְהָיוּ הַדְּבָרִים הָאֵלֶּה, V'hayu hadvarim ha·eileh,
אֲשֶׁר אָנֹכִי מְצַוְּךָ הַיּוֹם, asher anochi m'tzv'cha hayom,
עַל לְבָבֶךָ. al levavecha.
וְשִׁנַּנְתָּם לְבָנֶיךָ, וְדִבַּרְתָּ בָּם, V'shinantam levanecha, v'dibarta bam,
בְּשִׁבְתְּךָ בְּבֵיתֶךָ, וּבְלֶכְתְּךָ בַדֶּרֶךְ, b'shivt'cha b'veitecha, uvlecht'cha vaderech,
וּבְשָׁכְבְּךָ, וּבְקוּמֶךָ. uvshochb'cha, uvkumecha.
וּקְשַׁרְתָּם לְאוֹת עַל יָדֶךָ, Ukshartam l'ot al yadecha,
וְהָיוּ לְטֹטָפֹת בֵּין עֵינֶיךָ. v'hayu l'totafot bein einecha.
וּכְתַבְתָּם עַל מְזוּזוֹת בֵּיתֶךָ Uchtavtam al m'zuzot beitecha
וּבִשְׁעָרֶיךָ. uvisharecha.

Love the One, your God, with every heartbeat, with every breath,
with every conscious act.
Keep in mind the words I command you today.
Teach them to your children, talk about them at work;
whether you are tired or you are rested.
Let them guide the work of your hands;
keep them in the forefront of your vision.
Do not leave them at the doorway, or outside your gate.

וְהָיָה אִם שָׁמֹעַ תִּשְׁמְעוּ אֶל מִצְוֹתַי,	V'haya im shamo·a tishm'u el-mitzvotai,
אֲשֶׁר אָנֹכִי מְצַוֶּה אֶתְכֶם הַיּוֹם,	asher יהוה m'tzaveh etchem hayom,
לְאַהֲבָה אֶת יהוה אֱלֹהֵיכֶם וּלְעָבְדוֹ,	l'ahavah et יהוה eloheichem ulovdo,
בְּכָל לְבַבְכֶם וּבְכָל נַפְשְׁכֶם.	b'chol levavchem uvchol nafsh'chem.
וְנָתַתִּי מְטַר אַרְצְכֶם בְּעִתּוֹ,	V'natati m'tar artz'chem b'ito,
יוֹרֶה וּמַלְקוֹשׁ,	yoreh umalkosh,
וְאָסַפְתָּ דְגָנֶךָ וְתִירֹשְׁךָ וְיִצְהָרֶךָ.	v'asafta d'ganecha v'tirosh·cha v'yitz·harecha.
וְנָתַתִּי עֵשֶׂב בְּשָׂדְךָ לִבְהֶמְתֶּךָ,	v'natati eisev b'sad'cha livhemtecha,
וְאָכַלְתָּ וְשָׂבָעְתָּ.	v'achalta v'savata.
הִשָּׁמְרוּ לָכֶם פֶּן יִפְתֶּה לְבַבְכֶם,	Hishamru lachem pen yifteh levavchem,
וְסַרְתֶּם וַעֲבַדְתֶּם אֱלֹהִים אֲחֵרִים	v'sartem v'avadtem Elohim acheirim
וְהִשְׁתַּחֲוִיתֶם לָהֶם. וְחָרָה אַף יהוה בָּכֶם,	v'hishtachavitem lahem. V'chara af יהוה bachem,
וְעָצַר אֶת הַשָּׁמַיִם וְלֹא יִהְיֶה מָטָר,	v'atzar et hashamayim v'lo yiyeh matar,
וְהָאֲדָמָה לֹא תִתֵּן אֶת יְבוּלָהּ,	v'ha·adamah lo titen et-y'vulah;
וַאֲבַדְתֶּם מְהֵרָה מֵעַל הָאָרֶץ הַטֹּבָה	v'avad'tem m'heirah me·al ha·aretz hatovah
אֲשֶׁר יהוה נֹתֵן לָכֶם. וְשַׂמְתֶּם אֶת דְּבָרַי	asher יהוה notein lachem. V'samtem et-d'varai
אֵלֶּה עַל לְבַבְכֶם וְעַל נַפְשְׁכֶם,	eileh al levavchem v'al nafsh'chem,
וּקְשַׁרְתֶּם אֹתָם לְאוֹת עַל יֶדְכֶם,	ukshartem otam l'ot al-yedchem,
וְהָיוּ לְטוֹטָפֹת בֵּין עֵינֵיכֶם.	v'hayu l'totafot bein-eineichem.
וְלִמַּדְתֶּם אֹתָם אֶת בְּנֵיכֶם	V'limadtem otam et-b'neichem
לְדַבֵּר בָּם, בְּשִׁבְתְּךָ בְּבֵיתֶךָ,	ledabeir bam, b'shivt'cha b'veitecha,
וּבְלֶכְתְּךָ בַדֶּרֶךְ, וּבְשָׁכְבְּךָ,	uvlecht'cha vaderech, uvshochb'cha
וּבְקוּמֶךָ. וּכְתַבְתָּם עַל מְזוּזוֹת בֵּיתֶךָ	uv'kumecha. Uchtavtam al m'zuzot beitecha
וּבִשְׁעָרֶיךָ. לְמַעַן יִרְבּוּ יְמֵיכֶם	uvisharecha. L'ma·an yirbu y'meichem
וִימֵי בְנֵיכֶם עַל הָאֲדָמָה	vimei v'neichem al ha·adamah
אֲשֶׁר נִשְׁבַּע יהוה לַאֲבֹתֵיכֶם לָתֵת	asher nishba יהוה la·avoteichem lateit
לָהֶם, כִּימֵי הַשָּׁמַיִם עַל הָאָרֶץ.	lahem, kimei hashamayim alha·aretz.

How good it will be when you really listen and hear My directions which I give you today, to love יהוה who is your God and to act godly with feeling and inspiration. Your earthly needs will be met at the right time, appropriate to the season. You will reap what you have planted for your delight and health. Also your animals will have ample feed. All of you will eat and be content.

Be careful—watch out! Don't let your cravings delude you; don't become alienated; don't let your cravings become your gods; don't debase yourself to them because the God-sense within you will become distorted. Heaven will be shut to you, grace will not descend, Earth will not yield her produce. Your rushing will destroy you! And Earth will not be able to recover her good balance in which God's gifts manifest.

(translation: R' Zalman Schachter-Shalomi z"l)

MAARIV / EVENING PRAYER

וַיֹּאמֶר יהוה אֶל מֹשֶׁה לֵּאמֹר: Vayomer יהוה el-Moshe leimor:
דַּבֵּר אֶל בְּנֵי יִשְׂרָאֵל וְאָמַרְתָּ אֲלֵהֶם, Dabeir el b'nei Yisra·el v'amarta aleihem,
וְעָשׂוּ לָהֶם צִיצִת עַל כַּנְפֵי בִגְדֵיהֶם v'asu lahem tzitzit al kanfei bigdeihem
לְדֹרֹתָם, וְנָתְנוּ עַל צִיצִת הַכָּנָף ledorotam; v'natnu al tzitzit hakanaf
פְּתִיל תְּכֵלֶת. וְהָיָה לָכֶם לְצִיצִת, p'til t'cheilet. V'yaha lachem l'tzitzit,
וּרְאִיתֶם אֹתוֹ וּזְכַרְתֶּם אֶת כָּל מִצְוֹת uritem oto, uzchartem et-kol-mitzvot
יהוה, וַעֲשִׂיתֶם אֹתָם, וְלֹא תָתוּרוּ יהוה va·asitem otam. V'lo taturu
אַחֲרֵי לְבַבְכֶם וְאַחֲרֵי עֵינֵיכֶם, acharei levavchem v'acharei eineichem,
אֲשֶׁר אַתֶּם זֹנִים אַחֲרֵיהֶם. asher atem zonim achareihem.
לְמַעַן תִּזְכְּרוּ וַעֲשִׂיתֶם אֶת כָּל מִצְוֹתָי, Lema·an tizk'ru va·asitem et kol mitzvotai,
וִהְיִיתֶם קְדֹשִׁים לֵאלֹהֵיכֶם. vihyitem k'doshim leiloheichem.
אֲנִי יהוה אֱלֹהֵיכֶם, Ani יהוה eloheichem,
אֲשֶׁר הוֹצֵאתִי אֶתְכֶם מֵאֶרֶץ מִצְרַיִם, asher hotzeiti et·chem mei·eretz Mitzrayim,
לִהְיוֹת לָכֶם לֵאלֹהִים, liyot lachem le-Elohim:
אֲנִי יהוה אֱלֹהֵיכֶם. Ani יהוה eloheichem.

ה' Who Is said to Moshe:
"Speak, telling the *Yisrael* folks to make *tzitzit*
on the corners of their garments,
so they will have generations to follow them.
On each *tzitzit*-tassel let them set a blue thread.
Glance at it and in your seeing
remember all of the other directives of ה' who Is,
and act on them!
This way you will not be led astray,
craving to see and want,
and then prostitute yourself for your cravings.
This way you will be mindful to actualize my directions
for becoming dedicated to your God,
to be aware that I AM ה' who is your God —
the One who freed you from the oppression
in order to God you.
I am ה' your God."
This way you will be mindful to actualize my directions
for becoming dedicated to your God;
to be aware that I am your God,
the one who freed you from the oppression
in order to be your God. I am Adonai your God.
That is the truth!

(translation: R' Zalman Schachter-Shalomi z"l)

G'ulah: Redemption

אֱמֶת וֶאֱמוּנָה כָּל זֹאת, וְקַיָּם עָלֵינוּ,	Emet ve-emunah kol zot, v'kayam aleinu,
כִּי הוּא יהוה אֱלֹהֵינוּ וְאֵין זוּלָתוֹ,	ki hu יהוה Eloheinu v'ein zulato;
וַאֲנַחְנוּ יִשְׂרָאֵל עַמּוֹ.	va-anachnu Yisra·el amo.
הַפּוֹדֵנוּ מִיַּד מְלָכִים,	Hapodeinu miyad m'lachim,
מַלְכֵּנוּ הַגּוֹאֲלֵנוּ מִכַּף כָּל הֶעָרִיצִים.	malkeinu hago·aleinu mikaf kol he·aritzim.
הָאֵל הַנִּפְרָע לָנוּ מִצָּרֵינוּ,	Ha·El hanifra lanu mitzareinu,
וְהַמְשַׁלֵּם גְּמוּל לְכָל אֹיְבֵי נַפְשֵׁנוּ,	v'ham'shaleim g'mul l'chol oyvei nafsheinu,
הָעֹשֶׂה גְדוֹלוֹת עַד אֵין חֵקֶר,	haoseh g'dolot ad ein cheiker,
נִסִּים וְנִפְלָאוֹת עַד אֵין מִסְפָּר.	nisim v'niflaot ad ein mispar.
הַשָּׂם נַפְשֵׁנוּ בַּחַיִּים,	Hasam nafsheinu bachayim,
וְלֹא נָתַן לַמּוֹט רַגְלֵנוּ,	v'lo natan lamot ragleinu,
הַמַּדְרִיכֵנוּ עַל בָּמוֹת אוֹיְבֵינוּ,	hamadricheinu al bamot oyveinu,
וַיָּרֶם קַרְנֵנוּ עַל כָּל שׂוֹנְאֵינוּ.	v'yarem karneinu al kol soneinu.
הָעֹשֶׂה לָּנוּ נִסִּים וּנְקָמָה בְּפַרְעֹה,	Ha·oseh lanu nisim un'kamah b'Pharo,
אוֹתוֹת וּמוֹפְתִים בְּאַדְמַת בְּנֵי חָם,	otot umoftim b'admat b'nei cham,
וַיּוֹצֵא אֶת עַמּוֹ יִשְׂרָאֵל מִתּוֹכָם	v'yotzei et amo Yisra·el mitocham
לְחֵרוּת עוֹלָם.	l'cheirut olam.
הַמַּעֲבִיר בָּנָיו בֵּין גִּזְרֵי יַם סוּף,	Hama·avir banav bein gizrei yam suf,
וְרָאוּ בָנָיו גְּבוּרָתוֹ, שִׁבְּחוּ וְהוֹדוּ לִשְׁמוֹ.	v'ra·u vanav g'vurato, shibchu v'hodu lishmo.
וּמַלְכוּתוֹ בְּרָצוֹן קִבְּלוּ עֲלֵיהֶם,	U'malchuto b'ratzon kib'lu aleihem,
מֹשֶׁה וּמִרְיָם וּבְנֵי יִשְׂרָאֵל	Moshe uMiryam uvnei Yisra·el
לְךָ עָנוּ שִׁירָה בְּשִׂמְחָה רַבָּה,	l'cha anu shirah b'simchah rabah;
וְאָמְרוּ כֻלָּם:	v'am'ru chulam:

True and enduring, right and real, are these truths: that You, יהוה, are our God and there is none like You, and we, Israel / the God-wrestlers, are Your people.

You rescue us from the hands of kings and sovereigns. You are the God Who brought us forth from the Narrow Place and rescued us from the enemies of our souls. You are the One Who does great wonders and miracles beyond counting. You redeem us into life, and do not give us over into death. You lead us away from places and people of enmity toward us. You did signs and wonders for us before Pharaoh. Your might led to the death of the first-borns of Egypt as you led Your people Israel into freedom. You led us through the Sea of Reeds, and as everyone saw Your might we sang grateful praises to Your name.

Perceiving and accepting Your sovereignty, Moshe, Miryam, and all Israel sang this song to you in great joy, and together they said:

"Michamochah ba·eilim, יהוה? מִי כָמֹכָה בָּאֵלִם יהוה,
Mikamochah: nedar bakodesh, מִי כָּמֹכָה נֶאְדָּר בַּקֹּדֶשׁ,
nora t'hilot, oseih fele?" נוֹרָא תְהִלֹּת, עֹשֵׂה פֶלֶא.

Malchut'cha ra·u vanecha, מַלְכוּתְךָ רָאוּ בָנֶיךָ,
bokei·a yam lifnei Moshe uMiryam. בּוֹקֵעַ יָם לִפְנֵי מֹשֶׁה וּמִרְיָם,
"Zeh Eli!" anu; V'am'ru זֶה אֵלִי עָנוּ וְאָמְרוּ.
יהוה yimloch l'olam va·ed!" יהוה יִמְלֹךְ לְעוֹלָם וָעֶד.

V'ne·emar: "Ki fadah יהוה et Ya·akov; וְנֶאֱמַר. כִּי פָדָה יהוה אֶת יַעֲקֹב,
ug'alo miyad chazak mimenu." וּגְאָלוֹ מִיַּד חָזָק מִמֶּנּוּ.

Baruch atah, יהוה, ga·al Yisra·el. בָּרוּךְ אַתָּה יהוה, גָּאַל יִשְׂרָאֵל.

Who is like You, among the gods, יהוה?
Who is like You, awesome and doing wonders?

Your children saw your majesty, splitting the sea before Moses and Miryam.
"This is our God," they cried, "יהוה will reign through all space and time!"
And it is said: יהוה has saved the people of Jacob,
and redeems the weak from the mighty.

Blessed are You, יהוה, who redeems Israel.

Redemption

The Israelites walked into the Reed Sea
one foot at a time.
(What were they thinking about
  as the water rose
  up their legs
  chilling their hearts
  advancing toward their mouths?)

We continue to walk
here, now.
One foot at a time.
(On our better days, forward.)
 Alone
I
cannot reach the far shore
without drowning.

Somehow
I don't go under.
The person to my right
holds me up.
A still small voice
sustains him.

Blessed is the Source of Help
so often unexpected.
I step forward.
The sea is vast.

Blessed are You, Gracious One, for your unexpected moments of redemption.

(Mark Nazimova)

Hashkiveinu: Shelter of Peace

הַשְׁכִּיבֵנוּ יהוה אֱלֹהֵינוּ לְשָׁלוֹם,	Hashkiveinu יהוה Eloheinu, l'shalom;
וְהַעֲמִידֵנוּ מַלְכֵּנוּ לְחַיִּים טוֹבִים	v'ha·amideinu, malkeinu, l'chayim tovim
וּלְשָׁלוֹם, וּפְרֹשׂ עָלֵינוּ סֻכַּת שְׁלוֹמֶךָ,	ul'shalom, ufros aleinu sukkat sh'lomecha,
וְתַקְּנֵנוּ בְּעֵצָה טוֹבָה מִלְּפָנֶיךָ,	v'takneinu b'eitzah tovah milfanecha,
וְהוֹשִׁיעֵנוּ מְהֵרָה לְמַעַן שְׁמֶךָ.	v'hoshi·einu lema·an sh'mecha,
וְהָגֵן בַּעֲדֵנוּ, וְהָסֵר מֵעָלֵינוּ אוֹיֵב,	v'hagein ba·adeinu, v'haseir mei·aleinu oyeiv,
דֶּבֶר, וְחֶרֶב, וְרָעָב, וְיָגוֹן,	dever, v'cherev, v'ra·av v'yagon,
וְהָסֵר שָׂטָן מִלְּפָנֵינוּ וּמֵאַחֲרֵינוּ,	v'haseir satan milfaneinu umei·achareinu.
וּבְצֵל כְּנָפֶיךָ תַּסְתִּירֵנוּ.	Uv'tzeil k'nafecha tastireinu.
כִּי אֵל שׁוֹמְרֵנוּ וּמַצִּילֵנוּ אָתָּה,	Ki El shomreinu umatzileinu atah,
כִּי אֵל מֶלֶךְ חַנּוּן וְרַחוּם אָתָּה.	ki El Melech chanun v'rachum atah,
וּשְׁמֹר צֵאתֵנוּ וּבוֹאֵנוּ,	ushmor tzeiteinu uvo·einu,
לְחַיִּים וּלְשָׁלוֹם, מֵעַתָּה וְעַד עוֹלָם.	l'chayim ul'shalom, me·atah v'ad olam.
בָּרוּךְ אַתָּה יהוה,	Baruch atah יהוה,
שׁוֹמֵר עַמּוֹ יִשְׂרָאֵל לָעַד.	shomeir amo Yisra·el la·ad.

Help us to lie down in peace, יהוה our God, and to arise again to life.
Spread over the world Your sheltering peace.
Direct us with Your guidance and save us.
Protect and keep us from enmity, illness, violence, want, and sorrow.
Remove envy and recrimination from us;
help us to sidestep our internal adversary.
Shelter us in the shadow of Your wings, for You are a protecting, redeeming God.
You are God, our source of grace and mercy.
Guard our going out and our coming in, for life and for peace, now and forever.
Spread Your sheltering peace over us.
Blessed are You, יהוה, who spreads a shelter of peace over all of Your people.

from *Baruch* יהוה *L'Olam*: Blessed is the One Forever

בָּרוּךְ יהוה לְעוֹלָם, אָמֵן וְאָמֵן. Baruch יהוה l'olam, amen v'amen.
בָּרוּךְ יהוה מִצִּיּוֹן, Baruch יהוה miTziyon,
שֹׁכֵן יְרוּשָׁלַיִם הַלְלוּ־יָהּ. shochein Yerushalayim, Hal'lu·Yah.
בָּרוּךְ יהוה בַּיּוֹם, בָּרוּךְ יהוה בַּלָּיְלָה, Baruch יהוה bayom, baruch יהוה balailah,
בָּרוּךְ יהוה בְּשָׁכְבֵנוּ, baruch יהוה b'shochveinu,
בָּרוּךְ יהוה בְּקוּמֵנוּ. baruch יהוה b'kumeinu.
כִּי בְיָדְךָ נַפְשׁוֹת הַחַיִּים וְהַמֵּתִים, Ki v'yadcha nafshot hachayim v'hameitim,
אֲשֶׁר בְּיָדוֹ נֶפֶשׁ כָּל חָי asher b'yado nefesh kol chai
וְרוּחַ כָּל בְּשַׂר אִישׁ. v'ruach kol basar ish.
בְּיָדְךָ אַפְקִיד רוּחִי, פָּדִיתָה אוֹתִי, B'yadcha afkid ruchi, paditah oti,
יהוה, אֵל אֱמֶת. יהוה, El emet.

Blessed is the One forever, amen v'amen.
Blessed is the One dwelling in Zion and Jerusalem, halleluyah.

May the One be blessed by day and by night,
when we lie down and when we rise up.
For in Your hands are our lives and our deaths,
the breath of all life and the spirit of all flesh.
Into Your hands I place my spirit, O God of truth.

בָּרוּךְ אַתָּה יהוה, הַמֶּלֶךְ בִּכְבוֹדוֹ, Baruch atah יהוה, hamelech bichvodo,
תָּמִיד יִמְלֹךְ עָלֵינוּ לְעוֹלָם וָעֶד, tamid yimloch aleinu l'olam va·ed,
וְעַל כָּל מַעֲשָׂיו. v'al kol ma·asav.

Blessed are You, יהוה, who reigns in glory;
reign over us always, and over all of Your creations.

The Kaddish: A Door

In all of its forms, the Kaddish is a doorway
between one part of the service and the next.

As we move through this door, notice:
what is happening in your heart and mind?

Whatever is arising in you,
bring that into your prayer.

Chatzi Kaddish / Half Kaddish

יִתְגַּדַּל וְיִתְקַדַּשׁ שְׁמֵהּ רַבָּא. **Yitgadal v'yitkadash** sh'meih raba (**Amen**)
בְּעָלְמָא דִּי בְרָא כִרְעוּתֵהּ, b'alma di v'ra chiruteih,
וְיַמְלִיךְ מַלְכוּתֵהּ. v'yamlich malchuteih
בְּחַיֵּיכוֹן וּבְיוֹמֵיכוֹן b'chayeichon uvyomeichon,
וּבְחַיֵּי דְכָל בֵּית יִשְׂרָאֵל, uvchayei d'chol beit Yisra·el —
בַּעֲגָלָא וּבִזְמַן קָרִיב וְאִמְרוּ אָמֵן. ba·agala uvizman kariv; v'imru: **Amen.**

יְהֵא שְׁמֵהּ רַבָּא מְבָרַךְ **Y'hei sh'meih raba m'varach**
לְעָלַם וּלְעָלְמֵי עָלְמַיָּא. **l'alam ul·almei almaya.**

יִתְבָּרַךְ וְיִשְׁתַּבַּח וְיִתְפָּאַר Yitbarach v'yishtabach v'yitpa·ar
וְיִתְרוֹמַם וְיִתְנַשֵּׂא וְיִתְהַדָּר v'yit·romam v'yitnasei v'yit·hadar
וְיִתְעַלֶּה וְיִתְהַלָּל שְׁמֵהּ דְּקֻדְשָׁא v'yitaleh v'yit·halal sh'meih d'kudsha
בְּרִיךְ הוּא, brich Hu,
לְעֵלָּא l'eila

During the Ten Days of Repentance:
וּלְעֵלָּא uleila

מִן כָּל בִּרְכָתָא וְשִׁירָתָא, min kol birchata v'shirata,
תֻּשְׁבְּחָתָא וְנֶחֱמָתָא, tushb'chata v'nechemata,
דַּאֲמִירָן בְּעָלְמָא, da·amiran b'alma;
וְאִמְרוּ אָמֵן. v'imru: **Amen.**

Magnified and sanctified! Magnified and sanctified!
May God's Great Name fill the world God created.
May God's splendor be seen in the world in your life,
in your days, in the life of all Israel. Quickly and soon!
And let us say, **Amen.**

Forever may the Great Name be blessed!

Blessed and praised! Splendid and supreme!
May the holy Name, **Bless God**, be praised,
far beyond all the blessings and songs, comforts and consolations,
that can be offered in this world.
And let us say: **Amen.**

(Translated by Rabbi Daniel Brenner)

Weekday *Amidah*

Prelude to the Amidah

I hope these words
That come from me
Are words that come
From You
Through me.

(Rabbi David Zaslow)

In this service there are two versions of the weekday Amidah, the standing prayer that is at the heart of every Jewish service. First there is a contemplative version, in which we offer a kavanah or meditative focus for each of the Amidah's themes. Then there is the full-text version, which features the complete Hebrew text of the traditional prayer, and appears on p. 133.

Contemplative *Amidah*

Imahot v'Avot / Ancestors

I reflect on my ancestors. Who did I come from? How did they shape me?

Baruch atah יהוה, magein Avraham v'ezrat Sarah.
בָּרוּךְ אַתָּה יהוה, מָגֵן אַבְרָהָם וְעֶזְרַת שָׂרָה.

Gevurot / Power

What is the source of power in my life?
Where do I find strength? What enlivens me?

Baruch atah יהוה, m'chayei hameitim.
בָּרוּךְ אַתָּה יהוה, מְחַיֵּה הַמֵּתִים.

Kedushah / Holiness

I open myself to holiness. I seek to live wholly and in a way that is holy.

Baruch atah יהוה, ha·El hakadosh.
בָּרוּךְ אַתָּה יהוה, הָאֵל הַקָּדוֹשׁ.

Binah / Understanding

I seek wisdom and understanding in my life.

Baruch atah יהוה, chonein hada·at.
בָּרוּךְ אַתָּה יהוה, חוֹנֵן הַדָּעַת.

T'shuvah / Return

I want to orient myself in the right direction,
to re/turn to my deepest self and my highest aspirations.

Baruch atah יהוה, harotzeh bit·shuvah.
בָּרוּךְ אַתָּה יהוה, הָרוֹצֶה בִּתְשׁוּבָה.

Slicha / Forgiveness

I aspire to cultivate forgiveness,
and I ask all those whom I have hurt to forgive me.

Baruch atah יהוה, chanun hamarbeh lisloach.
בָּרוּךְ אַתָּה יהוה, חַנּוּן הַמַּרְבֶּה לִסְלֹחַ.

G'ulah / Redemption

I ask the source of transformation to lift me out of my narrow places.

Baruch atah יהוה, go·eil Yisra·el.
בָּרוּךְ אַתָּה יהוה, גּוֹאֵל יִשְׂרָאֵל.

Refu·ah / Healing

Heal my wounded places. Help me be a source of healing for others.

Baruch atah יהוה, rofei cholei amo Yisra·el.
בָּרוּךְ אַתָּה יהוה, רוֹפֵא חוֹלֵי עַמּוֹ יִשְׂרָאֵל.

Birkat HaShanim / Cycles

May abundant blessing pour into creation in this turning of the wheel
and in all of the cycles of our lives.

Baruch atah יהוה, m'varech hashanim.
בָּרוּךְ אַתָּה יהוה, מְבָרֵךְ הַשָּׁנִים.

Kibutz Galuyot / Ingathering

May we be gathered in from our spiritual exile.
May this be true for us as individuals and for us as a people.

Baruch atah יהוה, m'kabetz nidchei amo Yisra·el.
בָּרוּךְ אַתָּה יהוה, מְקַבֵּץ נִדְחֵי עַמּוֹ יִשְׂרָאֵל.

Din / Justice

May justice flow like waters
and righteousness like a mighty stream.
May we all be blessed with good judgment, discernment, and good boundaries.

Baruch atah יהוה, Melech oheiv tz'dakah umishpat.
בָּרוּךְ אַתָּה יהוה, מֶלֶךְ אוֹהֵב צְדָקָה וּמִשְׁפָּט.

Birkat Haminim / Divisions

May unhelpful divisions be bridged and healed.
May wickedness come to its end. May hope and righteousness reign.

Baruch atah יהוה, shoveir oyvim umachni·a zeidim.
בָּרוּךְ אַתָּה יהוה, שֹׁבֵר אֹיְבִים וּמַכְנִיעַ זֵדִים.

Tzaddikim / Righteous Ones

May all of my righteous and holy teachers be blessed.
May I recognize that the whole world can be my teacher.

Baruch atah יהוה, mishan umivtach latzadikim.
בָּרוּךְ אַתָּה יהוה, מִשְׁעָן וּמִבְטָח לַצַּדִּיקִים.

Binah Yerushalayim / Jerusalem

May Jerusalem, our holy city of old, be blessed with wholeness and peace.
May her inhabitants relate to one another with righteousness and love.
May all places where humanity dwells be blessed.

Baruch atah יהוה, boneih Yerushalayim.
בָּרוּךְ אַתָּה יהוה, בּוֹנֵה יְרוּשָׁלָיִם.

Yeshua / A World Transformed

May redemption flower forth and transform our world
into a world where suffering, hatred, and loss are no more.

Baruch atah יהוה, matzmiach keren y'shu·ah.
בָּרוּךְ אַתָּה יהוה, מַצְמִיחַ קֶרֶן יְשׁוּעָה.

Sh'ma Koleinu / Hear Our Voices

May our prayers be heard on high and deep within.
May the deepest murmurings of our hearts be heard and honored.

Baruch atah יהוה, shomei·a t'filah.
בָּרוּךְ אַתָּה יהוה, שׁוֹמֵעַ תְּפִלָּה.

Avoda / Service

May my life be an expression of my desire to serve something greater than myself.
May my service help to uplift Shechinah, Divine presence, everywhere.

Baruch atah יהוה, hamachazir shechinato l'tziyon.
בָּרוּךְ אַתָּה יהוה, הַמַּחֲזִיר שְׁכִינָתוֹ לְצִיּוֹן.

Hoda·a / Gratitude

Help me to cultivate gratitude for the blessings of every day.

Baruch atah יהוה, hatov shimcha ul'cha naeh l'hodot.
בָּרוּךְ אַתָּה יהוה, הַטּוֹב שִׁמְךָ וּלְךָ נָאֶה לְהוֹדוֹת.

Shalom / Peace

Help me to feel and to embody peace and wholeness.

Baruch atah יהוה, hamvareich et amo Yisra·el bashalom.
בָּרוּךְ אַתָּה יהוה, הַמְבָרֵךְ אֶת עַמּוֹ יִשְׂרָאֵל בַּשָּׁלוֹם.

עֹשֶׂה שָׁלוֹם בִּמְרוֹמָיו   Oseh shalom bimromav,
הוּא יַעֲשֶׂה שָׁלוֹם עָלֵינוּ   hu ya·aseh shalom aleinu
וְעַל כָּל יִשְׂרָאֵל,   v'al kol Yisra·el,
וְעַל כָּל יוֹשְׁבֵי תֵבֵל,   v'al kol yoshvei teiveil,
וְאִמְרוּ אָמֵן.   v'imru Amen.

May the One who makes peace in the heavens
make peace for us, for all Israel, and for all who dwell on earth.
And let us say: Amen.

Full Text *Amidah*

אֲדֹנָי שְׂפָתַי תִּפְתָּח Adonai s'fatai tiftach
וּפִי יַגִּיד תְּהִלָּתֶךָ. ufi yagid t'hilatecha.

Eternal God, open my lips
that my mouth may declare Your praise.

Avot v'imahot / Ancestors

בָּרוּךְ אַתָּה יהוה Baruch atah יהוה
אֱלֹהֵינוּ וֵאלֹהֵי אֲבוֹתֵינוּ Eloheinu v'Elohei avoteinu
וְאִמּוֹתֵינוּ, אֱלֹהֵי אַבְרָהָם, v'imoteinu, Elohei Avraham,
אֱלֹהֵי יִצְחָק, וֵאלֹהֵי יַעֲקֹב, Elohei Yitzchak, v'Elohei Ya·akov;

some omit

אֱלֹהֵי שָׂרָה, אֱלֹהֵי רִבְקָה, Elohei Sarah, Elohei Rivkah,
אֱלֹהֵי רָחֵל, וֵאלֹהֵי לֵאָה. Elohei Rachel v'Elohei Lei·ah,

הָאֵל הַגָּדוֹל הַגִּבּוֹר וְהַנּוֹרָא, Ha·El hagadol hagibor v'hanora,
אֵל עֶלְיוֹן, גּוֹמֵל חֲסָדִים טוֹבִים, El elyon, gomeil chasadim tovim
וְקֹנֵה הַכֹּל, v'koneih hakol,
וְזוֹכֵר חַסְדֵי אָבוֹת וְאִמָּהוֹת, v'zocheir chasdei avot v'imahot,
וּמֵבִיא גוֹאֵל לִבְנֵי בְנֵיהֶם, umeivi go·eil livnei v'neihem
לְמַעַן שְׁמוֹ בְּאַהֲבָה. l'ma·an sh'mo b'ahavah.

Blessed are You, יהוה our God and God of our ancestors,
God of Abraham, God of Isaac, God of Jacob;
God of Sarah, God of Rebecca, God of Rachel and God of Leah;
the great, mighty, and awesome God,
God on high,
who does deeds of loving kindness,
who is the Source of all,
and who remembers the steadfast love of our ancestors,
who lovingly brings redemption to their children's children
for Your name's sake.

MAARIV / EVENING PRAYER 134

> *During the Ten Days of T'shuvah (between Rosh Hashanah and Yom Kippur):*
>
> זָכְרֵנוּ לְחַיִּים, Zochreinu l'chayim,
> מֶלֶךְ חָפֵץ בַּחַיִּים, melech chafeitz bachayim,
> וְכָתְבֵנוּ בְּסֵפֶר הַחַיִּים, v'chotveinu b'sefer hachayim,
> לְמַעַנְךָ, אֱלֹהִים חַיִּים. l'ma·ancha, Elohim chayim.
>
> Remember us for life, Sovereign who chooses life, and inscribe us
> in the book of life for Your sake, God of life.

מֶלֶךְ עוֹזֵר וּמוֹשִׁיעַ וּמָגֵן. Melech ozeir umoshi·ah umagen.
בָּרוּךְ אַתָּה יהוה, מָגֵן אַבְרָהָם Baruch Atah יהוה, magein Avraham
וְעֶזְרַת שָׂרָה. v'ezrat Sarah.

Ruler, Helper, Redeemer, and Protector,
blessed are You, Abraham's shield and Sarah's strength.

Gevurot / Strength

אַתָּה גִּבּוֹר לְעוֹלָם יהוה, Atah gibor l'olam יהוה,
מְחַיֵּה מֵתִים אַתָּה, רַב לְהוֹשִׁיעַ. mechayeh meitim atah rav l'hoshi·ah.

Summer:
מוֹרִיד הַטָּל. Morid hatal.

Winter:
מַשִּׁיב הָרוּחַ וּמוֹרִיד הַגֶּשֶׁם. Mashiv haruach umorid hagashem.

You are our eternal strength, יהוה.
Your saving power gives life that transcends death.

Summer: You bring the dew of the field.
Winter: You cause the winds to blow & the rains to fall.

מְכַלְכֵּל חַיִּים בְּחֶסֶד, Mechalkeil chayim b'chesed,
מְחַיֵּה מֵתִים בְּרַחֲמִים רַבִּים, m'chayeih meitim b'rachamim rabim,
סוֹמֵךְ נוֹפְלִים, וְרוֹפֵא חוֹלִים, someich noflim, v'rofei cholim,
וּמַתִּיר אֲסוּרִים, umatir asurim,
וּמְקַיֵּם אֱמוּנָתוֹ לִישֵׁנֵי עָפָר. um'kayeim emunato lisheinei afar.
מִי כָמוֹךָ בַּעַל גְּבוּרוֹת Mi chamocha ba·al g'vurot?
וּמִי דוֹמֶה לָּךְ, Umi domeh lach?
מֶלֶךְ מֵמִית וּמְחַיֶּה Melech meimit um'chayeih,
וּמַצְמִיחַ יְשׁוּעָה. umatzmi·ach y'shu·ah.

You sustain the living with kindness,
in Your great mercy You bestow eternal life.
You support the fallen, heal the sick,
and free the captive.
You keep Your faith with us beyond life and death.
There is none like You, our source of strength,
the ruler of life and death, the source of our redemption.

During the Ten Days of T'shuvah (between Rosh Hashanah and Yom Kippur):

מִי כָמוֹךָ אַב הָרַחֲמִים, Mi chamocha av harachamim,
זוֹכֵר יְצוּרָיו לְחַיִּים בְּרַחֲמִים. zocheir y'tzurav l'chayim b'rachamim.

Who is like You, Source of Mercy,
Who mercifully remembers Your creatures for life?

וְנֶאֱמָן אַתָּה לְהַחֲיוֹת מֵתִים. V'ne·eman atah l'hachayot meitim.
בָּרוּךְ אַתָּה יהוה, מְחַיֵּה הַמֵּתִים. Baruch atah יהוה, m'chayeih hameitim.

Our faith is with You, the God Who brings eternal life.
Blessed are You, יהוה, Who gives life which transcends death.

Kidushat Hashem / Sanctification of God's Name

אַתָּה קָדוֹשׁ וְשִׁמְךָ קָדוֹשׁ, Atah kadosh v'shimcha kadosh
וּקְדוֹשִׁים בְּכָל יוֹם יְהַלְלוּךָ סֶּלָה. uk'doshim b'chol yom y'hal'lucha selah.
*בָּרוּךְ אַתָּה יהוה, הָאֵל הַקָּדוֹשׁ. *Baruch atah יהוה, ha·El hakadosh.

You are holy and Your name is holy
and holy ones praise You always.
Blessed* are You, יהוה, the holy God.

---

*During the Ten Days of T'shuvah

בָּרוּךְ אַתָּה, יהוה, הַמֶּלֶךְ הַקָּדוֹשׁ. Baruch atah, יהוה, ha·Melech hakadosh.

Blessed are You, יהוה, the holy King.

Bakashot / Weekday requests

אַתָּה חוֹנֵן לְאָדָם דַּעַת, Atah chonein l'adam da·at,
וּמְלַמֵּד לֶאֱנוֹשׁ בִּינָה. um'lamed le·enosh binah.
חָנֵּנוּ מֵאִתְּךָ חָכְמָה בִּינָה וָדָעַת. Choneinu mei·itcha chochmah binah vada·at.
בָּרוּךְ אַתָּה יהוה, חוֹנֵן הַדָּעַת. Baruch atah יהוה, chonein hada·at.

You give humanity wisdom and teach us understanding.
Grace us with wisdom, insight, and knowledge.
Blessed are You, יהוה, who graces us with wisdom.

הֲשִׁיבֵנוּ אָבִינוּ לְתוֹרָתֶךָ, Hashiveinu Avinu l'toratecha,
וְקָרְבֵנוּ מַלְכֵּנוּ לַעֲבוֹדָתֶךָ, v'korveinu Malkeinu la·avodatecha,
וְהַחֲזִירֵנוּ בִּתְשׁוּבָה שְׁלֵמָה לְפָנֶיךָ. בָּ v'hachazireinu bit·shuvah sh'leimah l'fanecha.
רוּךְ אַתָּה יהוה, הָרוֹצֶה בִּתְשׁוּבָה. Baruch atah יהוה, harotzeih bit·shuvah.

Return us, our Parent, to Your Torah; draw us near, our Sovereign, to Your service;
help us to return in complete *t'shuvah* before You.
Blessed are You, יהוה, who wishes for our *t'shuvah*.

סְלַח לָנוּ, אָבִינוּ, כִּי חָטָאנוּ,   S'lach lanu, Avinu, ki chatanu;
מְחַל לָנוּ, מַלְכֵּנוּ, כִּי פָשָׁעְנוּ,   m'chal lanu, Malkeinu, ki fashanu;
כִּי אֵל טוֹב וְסַלָּח אָתָּה.   ki El tov v'solei·ach atah.
בָּרוּךְ אַתָּה יהוה,   Baruch atah יהוה,
חַנּוּן הַמַּרְבֶּה לִסְלֹחַ.   chanun hamarbeh lislo·ach.

Forgive us, our Parent, for we have sinned;
pardon us, our Sovereign, for we have erred;
for You are the one who forgives and pardons.
Blessed are You, יהוה, who graciously forgives.

רְאֵה נָא בְעָנְיֵנוּ, וְרִיבָה רִיבֵנוּ,   R'eih na v'an·yeinu, v'rivah riveinu,
וּגְאָלֵנוּ גְּאֻלָּה שְׁלֵמָה   ug'aleinu g'ulah sh'leimah
מְהֵרָה לְמַעַן שְׁמֶךָ,   m'heirah l'ma·an sh'mecha,
כִּי אֵל גּוֹאֵל חָזָק אָתָּה.   ki El go·eil chazak atah.
בָּרוּךְ אַתָּה יהוה, גּוֹאֵל יִשְׂרָאֵל.   Baruch atah יהוה, go·eil Yisra·el.

Take note of our affliction and our struggles.
Redeem us swiftly for Your name's sake. Blessed are You, יהוה, Redeemer of Israel.

רְפָאֵנוּ, יהוה, וְנֵרָפֵא,   R'fa·einu, יהוה, v'neirafei;
הוֹשִׁיעֵנוּ וְנִוָּשֵׁעָה,   hoshieinu v'nivasheiah,
כִּי תְהִלָּתֵנוּ אָתָּה,   ki t'hilateinu atah,
וְהַעֲלֵה רְפוּאָה שְׁלֵמָה לְכָל מַכּוֹתֵינוּ.   v'ha·aleih refu·ah sh'leimah l'chol makoteinu.
כִּי אֵל מֶלֶךְ רוֹפֵא נֶאֱמָן וְרַחֲמָן אָתָּה.   Ki El Melech rofei ne·eman v'rachaman atah.
בָּרוּךְ אַתָּה יהוה,   Baruch atah יהוה,
רוֹפֵא חוֹלֵי עַמּוֹ יִשְׂרָאֵל.   rofei cholei amo Yisra·el.

Heal us, יהוה, and we will be healed; save us, and let us be saved;
for You are the healer, and from You complete healing rises for every wound.
Blessed are You, יהוה, healer of the sick among Your people.

בָּרֵךְ עָלֵינוּ, יהוה אֱלֹהֵינוּ, Bareich aleinu, יהוה Eloheinu,
אֶת הַשָּׁנָה הַזֹּאת et hashanah hazot
וְאֶת כָּל מִינֵי תְבוּאָתָהּ לְטוֹבָה, v'et kol minei t'vuatah l'tovah

summer: וְתֵן בְּרָכָה   summer: v'tein b'racha
winter: וְתֵן טַל וּמָטָר לִבְרָכָה   winter: v'tein tal umatar livracha

עַל פְּנֵי הָאֲדָמָה, וְשַׂבְּעֵנוּ מִטּוּבָהּ, al p'nei ha·adamah, v'sabeinu mituvah,
וּבָרֵךְ שְׁנָתֵנוּ כַּשָּׁנִים הַטּוֹבוֹת לִבְרָכָה, uvareich sh'nateinu kashanim hatovot
כִּי אֵל טוֹב וּמֵטִיב אַתָּה, livracha, ki El tov-umeitiv atah,
וּמְבָרֵךְ הַשָּׁנִים. umvareich hashanim.
בָּרוּךְ אַתָּה יהוה, מְבָרֵךְ הַשָּׁנִים. Baruch atah יהוה, m'vareich hashanim.

Bless, יהוה our God, the cycle of this year
and all the various good things which grow.

in summer: Grant blessing
in winter: Grant the blessing of the dew

on the face of the earth.
Satisfy us with Your goodness, and bless this year as all good years.
Blessed are You, יהוה, who blesses the cycle of the years.

תְּקַע בְּשׁוֹפָר גָּדוֹל לְחֵרוּתֵנוּ, T'ka b'shofar gadol l'cheiruteinu,
וְשָׂא נֵס לְקַבֵּץ גָּלֻיּוֹתֵינוּ, v'sa neis l'kabetz galuyoteinu,
וְקַבְּצֵנוּ יַחַד מְהֵרָה v'kabtzeinu yachad m'heirah
מֵאַרְבַּע כַּנְפוֹת הָאָרֶץ לְאַרְצֵנוּ. mei·arba kanfot ha·aretz l'artzeinu.
בָּרוּךְ אַתָּה יהוה, Baruch atah יהוה,
מְקַבֵּץ נִדְחֵי עַמּוֹ יִשְׂרָאֵל. m'kabeitz nidchei amo Yisra·el.

Sound the great shofar for our freedom,
raise a banner for the oppressed, gather us in from the four corners of the earth.
Blessed are You, יהוה, who ingathers the exiles of Your people.

הָשִׁיבָה שׁוֹפְטֵינוּ כְּבָרִאשׁוֹנָה Hashivah shofteinu k'varishonah
וְיוֹעֲצֵינוּ כְּבַתְּחִלָּה, v'yo·atzeinu k'vat·chilah,
וְהָסֵר מִמֶּנּוּ יָגוֹן וַאֲנָחָה, v'haseir mimenu yagon va·anachah,
וּמְלוֹךְ עָלֵינוּ מְהֵרָה אַתָּה, יהוה, umloch aleinu m'heirah atah, יהוה,
לְבַדְּךָ בְּחֶסֶד וּבְרַחֲמִים, l'vadcha b'chesed uvrachamim,
וְצַדְּקֵנוּ בְּצֶדֶק וּבְמִשְׁפָּט. v'tzadkeinu b'tzedek uv'mishpat.
בָּרוּךְ אַתָּה יהוה, Baruch atah יהוה,
מֶלֶךְ אוֹהֵב צְדָקָה וּמִשְׁפָּט. Melech oheiv tz'dakah umishpat.

Let our judges be righteous, as they were of old;
bring mercy and lovingkindness through them;
for You are our ultimate ruler,
You alone in Your mercy and compassion, your justice and your statutes.
Blessed are You, יהוה, Ruler who loves justice.

וְלַמַּלְשִׁינוּת אַל תְּהִי תִקְוָה, V'lamalshinut al t'hi tikvah,
וְכָל הַמִּינִים כְּרֶגַע יֹאבֵדוּ, v'chol haminim k'rega yoveidu,
וְכָל אוֹיְבֵי עַמְּךָ מְהֵרָה יִכָּרֵתוּ, v'chol oyvei amcha m'heirah y'kareitu,
וְהַזֵּדִים מְהֵרָה תְעַקֵּר וּתְשַׁבֵּר v'hazeidim m'heirah t'akeir ut·shabeir
וּתְמַגֵּר וּתְכַלֵּם וְתַשְׁפִּילֵם utmageir utchalem v'tashpilim
וְתַכְנִיעֵם בִּמְהֵרָה בְיָמֵינוּ. v'tachni·eim bimheirah v'yameinu.
בָּרוּךְ אַתָּה יהוה, Baruch atah יהוה,
שׁוֹבֵר אוֹיְבִים וּמַכְנִיעַ זֵדִים. shoveir oyvim umachnia zeidim.

And may wickedness not be given hope,
and may the errant return to You, speedily and in our days.
Blessed are You, יהוה, who shatters wickedness.

עַל הַצַּדִּיקִים וְעַל הַחֲסִידִים	Al hatzadikim v'al hachasidim
וְעַל זִקְנֵי עַמְּךָ בֵּית יִשְׂרָאֵל,	v'al ziknei amcha beit Yisra·el,
וְעַל פְּלֵיטַת סוֹפְרֵיהֶם,	v'al pleitat sofreihem,
וְעַל גֵּרֵי הַצֶּדֶק וְעָלֵינוּ,	v'al gerei hatzedek v'aleinu,
יֶהֱמוּ נָא רַחֲמֶיךָ, יהוה אֱלֹהֵינוּ,	yehemu na rachamecha יהוה Eloheinu,
וְתֵן שָׂכָר טוֹב	v'tein sachar tov
לְכָל הַבּוֹטְחִים בְּשִׁמְךָ בֶּאֱמֶת,	l'chol habotchim b'shimcha b'emet,
וְשִׂים חֶלְקֵנוּ עִמָּהֶם,	v'sim chelkeinu imahem,
וּלְעוֹלָם לֹא נֵבוֹשׁ כִּי בְךָ בָּטָחְנוּ,	ul'olam lo neivosh ki v'cha batachnu,
וְעַל חַסְדְּךָ הַגָּדוֹל בֶּאֱמֶת נִשְׁעָנּוּ.	v'al chasd'cha hagadol be·emet nishan'nu.
בָּרוּךְ אַתָּה יהוה,	Baruch atah יהוה,
מִשְׁעָן וּמִבְטָח לַצַּדִּיקִים.	mishan umivtach latzadikim.

And on the righteous ones and the pious ones and our elders,
and on our leaders, and on the strangers who dwell among us, and on us,
may you grant compassion, יהוה our God,
and give blessing and good reward to all who trust in Your name,
and number us among them forever, and let us never waver from our faith in You.
Blessed are You, יהוה, the staff and stay of the righteous.

וְלִירוּשָׁלַיִם עִירְךָ בְּרַחֲמִים תָּשׁוּב,	V'liYerushalayim ircha b'rachamim tashuv,
וְתִשְׁכּוֹן בְּתוֹכָהּ כַּאֲשֶׁר דִּבַּרְתָּ,	v'tishkon b'tochah ka·asher dibarta,
וּבְנֵה אוֹתָהּ בְּקָרוֹב בְּיָמֵינוּ	uvneih otah b'karov b'yameinu
בִּנְיַן עוֹלָם,	binyan olam,
וְכִסֵּא דָוִד עַבְדְּךָ	v'chisei David avd'cha
מְהֵרָה לְתוֹכָהּ תָּכִין.	m'heirah l'tochah tachin.
בָּרוּךְ אַתָּה יהוה, בּוֹנֵה יְרוּשָׁלָיִם.	Baruch atah, יהוה, boneih Yerushalayim.

And to Jerusalem Your city speedily return in compassion.
Help us to rebuild her speedily and in our days,
in a manner befitting the throne of David.
Give rest to Zion and help us to rebuild Jerusalem.
Blessed are You, יהוה, builder of Jerusalem.

אֶת צֶמַח דָּוִד עַבְדְּךָ	Et tzemach David avd'cha
מְהֵרָה תַצְמִיחַ,	m'heirah tatzmiach,
וְקַרְנוֹ תָּרוּם בִּישׁוּעָתֶךָ,	v'karno tarum bishu·atecha,
כִּי לִישׁוּעָתְךָ קִוִּינוּ כָּל הַיּוֹם.	ki lishu·atecha kivinu kol hayom.
בָּרוּךְ אַתָּה יהוה,	Baruch atah יהוה,
מַצְמִיחַ קֶרֶן יְשׁוּעָה.	matzmiach keren y'shu·ah.

May the sprout of David flower forth,
bringing with it Your redemption, for we hope for Your redemption every day.
Blessed are You, יהוה, who brings forth redemption.

שְׁמַע קוֹלֵנוּ, יהוה אֱלֹהֵינוּ,	Sh'ma koleinu, יהוה Eloheinu,
חוּס וְרַחֵם עָלֵינוּ,	chus v'racheim aleinu,
וְקַבֵּל בְּרַחֲמִים וּבְרָצוֹן אֶת	v'kabeil b'rachamim uvratzon et t'filateinu,
תְּפִלָּתֵנוּ,	ki El shome·a t'filot v'tachanunim atah,
כִּי אֵל שׁוֹמֵעַ תְּפִלּוֹת וְתַחֲנוּנִים	umilfaneicha, malkeinu, reikam al
אָתָּה, וּמִלְּפָנֶיךָ, מַלְכֵּנוּ, רֵיקָם אַל	tashiveinu, chaneinu v'aneinu ushma
תְּשִׁיבֵנוּ,	t'filateinu.
חָנֵּנוּ וַעֲנֵנוּ וּשְׁמַע תְּפִלָּתֵנוּ.	Ki atah shome·a
כִּי אַתָּה שׁוֹמֵעַ	t'filat kol peh b'rachamim.
תְּפִלַּת כָּל פֶּה בְּרַחֲמִים.	Baruch atah, יהוה, shome·a t'filah.
בָּרוּךְ אַתָּה יהוה, שׁוֹמֵעַ תְּפִלָּה.	

Hear our words, יהוה our God,
be compassionate and merciful upon us,
and let our prayers be received with mercy according to Your will,
for You are the one who hears our prayers and supplications
which arise before You.
You are the one who hears the prayers of all lips with compassion.
Blessed are You, יהוה, hearer of prayer.

רְצֵה, יהוה אֱלֹהֵינוּ, בְּעַמְּךָ יִשְׂרָאֵל,	R'tzeih, יהוה Eloheinu, b'amcha Yisra·el,
וְלִתְפִלָּתָם שְׁעֵה,	v'litfilatam sh'eih,
וְהָשֵׁב אֶת הָעֲבוֹדָה לִדְבִיר בֵּיתֶךָ,	v'hasheiv et ha·avoda lidvir beitecha,
וְאִשֵּׁי יִשְׂרָאֵל, וּתְפִלָּתָם	v'ishei Yisra·el, utfilatam
מְהֵרָה בְּאַהֲבָה תְקַבֵּל בְּרָצוֹן,	m'heirah b'ahavah t'kabel b'ratzon,
וּתְהִי לְרָצוֹן תָּמִיד	ut'hi l'ratzon tamid
עֲבוֹדַת יִשְׂרָאֵל עַמֶּךָ.	avodat Yisra·el amecha.
וְתֶחֱזֶינָה עֵינֵינוּ בְּשׁוּבְךָ	V'techezenah eineinu b'shuvcha
לְצִיּוֹן בְּרַחֲמִים. בָּרוּךְ אַתָּה יהוה,	l'tziyon b'rachamim. Baruch atah, יהוה,
הַמַּחֲזִיר שְׁכִינָתוֹ לְצִיּוֹן.	hamachazir shechinato l'tziyon.

Accept, יהוה our God, the prayers of Your people Israel;
find favor in us and accept our prayers in love.
May our prayers always ascend to You in love.
And help our eyes and hearts to behold Your return to Zion with compassion.
Blessed are You, יהוה, whose Presence returns always to Zion.

On Rosh Chodesh, and on the intermediate days of festivals:

אֱלֹהֵינוּ וֵאלֹהֵי אֲבוֹתֵינוּ וְאִמּוֹתֵינוּ,	Eloheinu v'Elohei avoteinu v'imoteinu,
יַעֲלֶה וְיָבֹא, וְיַגִּיעַ, וְיֵרָאֶה,	ya·aleh v'yavo, v'yagia, v'yeira·eh,
וְיֵרָצֶה, וְיִשָּׁמַע, וְיִפָּקֵד,	v'yeiratzeh, v'yishama, v'yipakeid,
וְיִזָּכֵר זִכְרוֹנֵנוּ וּפִקְדוֹנֵנוּ,	v'yizacheir zichroneinu ufikdoneinu,
וְזִכְרוֹן אֲבוֹתֵינוּ וְאִמּוֹתֵינוּ,	v'zichron avoteinu v'imoteinu,
וְזִכְרוֹן מָשִׁיחַ בֶּן דָּוִד עַבְדֶּךָ,	v'zichron mashi·ach ben David avdecha,
וְזִכְרוֹן יְרוּשָׁלַיִם עִיר קָדְשֶׁךָ,	vzichron Yerushalayim ir kodshecha,
וְזִכְרוֹן כָּל עַמְּךָ בֵּית יִשְׂרָאֵל לְפָנֶיךָ,	v'zichron kol amcha beit Yisra·el l'fanecha,
לִפְלֵיטָה, לְטוֹבָה,	lifleitah, l'tovah,
לְחֵן וּלְחֶסֶד וּלְרַחֲמִים,	l'chein ulchesed ulrachamim,
לְחַיִּים וּלְשָׁלוֹם, בְּיוֹם:	l'chayim ulshalom, b'yom:

רֹאשׁ הַחֹדֶשׁ הַזֶּה	לְרֹאשׁ־חֹדֶשׁ:	Rosh Chodesh:	Rosh haChodesh hazeh
חַג הַמַּצּוֹת הַזֶּה	לְפֶסַח:	Pesach:	Chag haMatzot hazeh
חַג הַסֻּכּוֹת הַזֶּה	לְסֻכּוֹת:	Sukkot:	Chag haSukkot hazeh

זָכְרֵנוּ, יְיָ, אֱלֹהֵינוּ, בּוֹ לְטוֹבָה,	Zochreinu, יהוה Eloheinu, bo l'tovah,
וּפָקְדֵנוּ בוֹ לִבְרָכָה,	u'fakdeinu bo livracha,
וְהוֹשִׁיעֵנוּ בוֹ לְחַיִּים,	v'hoshiyeinu bo l'chayim,
וּבִדְבַר יְשׁוּעָה וְרַחֲמִים,	uvidvar y'shu·ah v'rachamim,
חוּס וְחָנֵּנוּ,	chus v'chaneinu,
וְרַחֵם עָלֵינוּ וְהוֹשִׁיעֵנוּ,	v'rachem aleinu v'hoshiyeinu,
כִּי אֵלֶיךָ עֵינֵינוּ,	ki eilecha eineinu,
כִּי אֵל מֶלֶךְ חַנּוּן וְרַחוּם אָתָּה.	ki El Melech chanun v'rachum atah.

On Rosh Chodesh, and on the intermediate days of festivals:

Our God and God of our ancestors:
allow memory to ascend,
to come, to reach us.
May our memory
and our ancestors' memory,
and the memory of the dream
of a messianic time,
and the memory of the vision
of Jerusalem as a city of peace,
and the memories of all of Your people
of the House of Israel,
be before You

on this day of (Rosh Chodesh) (Pesach) (Sukkot)

On this day
may these memories,
these dreams of redemption,
inspire graciousness, lovingkindness,
and compassion in us,
for life and for peace.
Remember us, יהוה our God, for goodness.
Count us in for blessing.
Save us with life.
Shower us with salvation
and with compassion;
be merciful to us; enfold us
in the compassion we knew
before we were born.
For You are our merciful parent and sovereign.

מוֹדִים אֲנַחְנוּ לָךְ, שָׁאַתָּה הוּא,	Modim anachnu lach, she·atah hu,
יהוה אֱלֹהֵינוּ וֵאלֹהֵי אֲבוֹתֵינוּ,	יהוה Eloheinu v'Elohei avoteinu,
וְאִמּוֹתֵינוּ,	v'imoteinu,
לְעוֹלָם וָעֶד, צוּרֵנוּ צוּר חַיֵּינוּ,	l'olam va·ed, tzureinu tzur chayeinu,
מָגֵן יִשְׁעֵנוּ,	magen yisheinu,
אַתָּה הוּא לְדוֹר וָדוֹר,	atah hu l'dor vador,
נוֹדֶה לְךָ וּנְסַפֵּר תְּהִלָּתֶךָ,	nodeh lecha unsaper t'hilatecha,
עַל חַיֵּינוּ הַמְּסוּרִים בְּיָדֶךָ,	al chayeinu hamsurim b'yadecha,
וְעַל נִשְׁמוֹתֵינוּ הַפְּקוּדוֹת לָךְ,	v'al nishmoteinu hapkudot lach,
וְעַל נִסֶּיךָ שֶׁבְּכָל יוֹם עִמָּנוּ,	v'al nisecha sheb'chol yom imanu,
וְעַל נִפְלְאוֹתֶיךָ וְטוֹבוֹתֶיךָ	v'al nifl'otecha v'tovotecha
שֶׁבְּכָל עֵת, עֶרֶב וָבֹקֶר וְצָהֳרָיִם,	sheb'chol eit, erev vavoker v'tzohorayim.
הַטּוֹב, כִּי לֹא כָלוּ רַחֲמֶיךָ,	Hatov, ki lo chalu rachamecha;
וְהַמְרַחֵם, כִּי לֹא תַמּוּ חֲסָדֶיךָ:	v'hamracheim, ki lo tamu chasadecha:
כִּי מֵעוֹלָם קִוִּינוּ לָךְ.	ki mei·olam kivinu lach.

We are grateful before You,
for You, יהוה our God and God of our ancestors, are forever
the rock of our lives, the shield of our salvation.
You are this for us in every generation.
For our lives which are in Your hands,
and our souls which are in Your keeping,
and for the wonders You do for us each day
and the miracles You perform for us at every moment,
evening and morning and afternoon:
Your mercies never end,
Your compassion never fails;
we put our hope in You.

On Chanukah and Purim:

עַל הַנִּסִּים, וְעַל הַפֻּרְקָן, Al hanisim, v'al hapurkan,
וְעַל הַגְּבוּרוֹת, וְעַל הַתְּשׁוּעוֹת, v'al hagvurot, v'al hat'shu·ot,
וְעַל הַנִּפְלָאוֹת, v'al hanifla·ot,
שֶׁעָשִׂיתָ לַאֲבוֹתֵינוּ וּלְאִמּוֹתֵינוּ she·asita la·avoteinu ulimoteinu
בַּיָּמִים הָהֵם בַּזְּמַן הַזֶּה. bayamim haheim bazman hazeh.

For the miracles, for the redemption,
for the mighty deeds, for the saving acts,
and for the wonders which You wrought for our ancestors
in those days, at this time:

On Chanukah:

בִּימֵי מַתִּתְיָהוּ כֹּהֵן גָּדוֹל Bimei Mattityahu cohein gadol
חַשְׁמוֹנָאִי וּבָנָיו כְּשֶׁעָמְדָה עֲלֵיהֶם chashmona·i uvanav k'sh'amdah aleihem
מַלְכוּת אַנְטִיּוֹכוֹס הָרָשָׁע malchut Antiochos harasha
וּבִקֵּשׁ לַעֲקֹר אֶת אֱמוּנָתֵנוּ uvikeish la·akor et emunateinu
וְדָתֵנוּ וְהֵצֵרוּ לָנוּ וְכָבְשׁוּ אֶת v'dateinu v'heitzeiru lanu v'chavshu et
הֵיכָלֵנוּ, טִמְּאוּ אֶת מִקְדָּשֵׁנוּ. heichaleinu, timu et mikdasheinu.
אָז קָמוּ נֶגְדָּם חֲסִידֶיךָ Az kamu negdam chasidecha
וְכֹהֲנֶיךָ וְאַתָּה בְּרַחֲמֶיךָ v'chohanecha v'atah b'rachamecha
הָרַבִּים, עָמַדְתָּ לָהֶם בְּעֵת צָרָתָם, harabim, amad'ta lahem b'eit tzaratam,
רַבְתָּ אֶת רִיבָם, נָקַמְתָּ אֶת נִקְמָתָם ravta et rivam, nakamta et nikmatam
וְהָיִיתָ בְּעֶזְרָתָם לְהִתְגַּבֵּר עֲלֵיהֶם v'ha·yita b'ezratam l'hitgabeir aleihem
וּלְטַהֵר אֶת הַמִּקְדָּשׁ. ul'taheir et hamikdash.
מִתּוֹךְ גַּעֲגוּעִים לְהַשְׁרָאָתְךָ Mitoch gagu·im l'hashra·at'cha
רָצוּ לְהַדְלִיק אֶת הַמְּנוֹרָה ratzu l'hadlik et hamenorah
הַטְּהוֹרָה וְלֹא מָצְאוּ שֶׁמֶן hat'horah v'lo matzu shemen
עַד שֶׁהוֹרֵית לָהֶם שֶׁמֶן טָהוֹר ad shehoreita lahem shemen tahor
לְיוֹם אֶחָד. בְּבִטָּחוֹן הִדְלִיקוּ אֶת l'yom echad. B'vitachon hidliku et
הַמְּנוֹרָה וְאַתָּה עָשִׂיתָ לָהֶם נֵס וָפֶלֶא haMenorah v'atah asita lahem neis vafeleh
וְהַשֶּׁמֶן לֹא הִפְסִיק עַד שֶׁעָשׂוּ מֵחָדָשׁ. v'hashemen lo hifsik ad she·asu meichadash.
וְקָבְעוּ שְׁמוֹנַת יְמֵי חֲנֻכָּה אֵלּוּ V'kavu shmonat y'mei Chanukah eilu
לְהַדְלִיק נֵרוֹת לְפִרְסוּם הַנֵּס לְהוֹדוֹת l'hadlik neirot l'firsum haneis l'hodot
בְּהַלֵּל לְשִׁמְךָ הַגָּדוֹל וְהַקָּדוֹשׁ עַל b'halel l'shimcha hagadol v'hakadosh al
נִסֶּיךָ וְעַל נִפְלְאוֹתֶיךָ וְעַל יְשׁוּעָתֶיךָ. nisecha v'al nifl'otecha v'al y'shu·atecha.

On Chanukah:

In the days of Mattityahu, High priest, and his sons, when there arose against them the reign of wicked Antiochus who sought to uproot our faith and law, oppressing us, they conquered our Temple and desecrated our sanctuary.

Then there arose, against them, Your devout priests, and You, in Your great compassion, stood by them, in their troubles, waging their wars, avenging their pain, helping them to overcome Antiochus' forces and to purify the sanctuary. Amidst their longing for Your Presence among them, they sought to kindle the pure lamps and, not finding enough pure oil, You led them to find some, just enough for one day. In trust, they kindled the Lamp, and You miraculously made the oil last until they could make some afresh. Then did they set these days of Chanukah to lighting candles, to chanting the Hallel, in gratitude to Your great reputation for Your miracles, Your wonders and Your salvation.

(adaptation and translation: R' Zalman Schachter-Shalomi z"l)

On Purim:

בִּימֵי מָרְדְּכַי וְאֶסְתֵּר בְּשׁוּשַׁן	Bimei Mordechai v'Ester b'Shushan
הַבִּירָה, כְּשֶׁעָמַד עֲלֵיהֶם הָמָן	habirah, k'she·amad aleihem Haman
הָרָשָׁע, בִּקֵּשׁ לְהַשְׁמִיד,	harasha, bikeish l'hashmid,
לַהֲרֹג וּלְאַבֵּד אֶת כָּל הַיְּהוּדִים,	l'harog ul'abeid et kol ha·y'hudim,
מִנַּעַר וְעַד זָקֵן, טַף וְנָשִׁים,	mina·ar v'ad zakein, taf v'nashim,
בְּיוֹם אֶחָד בִּשְׁלֹשָׁה עָשָׂר	b'yom echad bishlosha asar
לְחֹדֶשׁ שְׁנֵים עָשָׂר,	l'chodesh shneim asar,
הוּא חֹדֶשׁ אֲדָר, וּשְׁלָלָם לָבוֹז.	hu chodesh Adar, ushlalam lavoz.
וְאַתָּה בְּרַחֲמֶיךָ הָרַבִּים	V'atah b'rachamecha harabim
הֵפַרְתָּ אֶת עֲצָתוֹ,	heifarta et atzato,
וְקִלְקַלְתָּ אֶת מַחֲשַׁבְתּוֹ,	v'kilkalta et mach·shavto,
וַהֲשֵׁבוֹתָ לוֹ גְּמוּלוֹ בְּרֹאשׁוֹ.	vahasheivota lo g'mulo b'rosho.

In the days of Mordechai and Esther in Shushan, the capital, when the wicked Haman arose before them and sought to destroy, to slay, and to exterminate all the Jews — young and old, infants and women — on the same day, the thirteenth of the twelfth month, which is the month of Adar, and to plunder their possessions: You, in Your abundant mercy, nullified his counsel and frustrated his intention and caused his design to return upon his own head.

וְעַל כֻּלָּם יִתְבָּרַךְ וְיִתְרוֹמַם V'al kulam yitbarach v'yit·romam
שִׁמְךָ מַלְכֵּנוּ shimcha Malkeinu
תָּמִיד לְעוֹלָם וָעֶד. tamid l'olam va·ed.

For all these things, O God, let Your name forever be praised.

During the Ten Days of Repentance:

וּכְתֹב לְחַיִּים טוֹבִים כָּל בְּנֵי בְרִיתֶךָ, Uchtov l'chayim tovim kol b'nei v'ritecha.
May all the children of Your covenant be inscribed for a life of goodness.

וְכֹל הַחַיִּים יוֹדוּךָ סֶּלָה, v'chol hachayim yoducha selah,
וִיהַלְלוּ אֶת שִׁמְךָ vihal'lu et shimcha
בֶּאֱמֶת, be·emet,
הָאֵל יְשׁוּעָתֵנוּ וְעֶזְרָתֵנוּ סֶלָה. ha·El y'shu·ateinu v'ezrateinu selah.
בָּרוּךְ אַתָּה, יהוה, Baruch atah, יהוה,
הַטּוֹב שִׁמְךָ וּלְךָ נָאֶה לְהוֹדוֹת. hatov shimcha ulcha na·eh l'hodot.

For You are the God of our redemption and our hope.
Blessed are You, יהוה, whose Name is good
and who does great things worthy of our thanksgiving.

Shalom / Peace

שָׁלוֹם רָב עַל יִשְׂרָאֵל עַמְּךָ Shalom rav al Yisra·el am'cha
תָּשִׂים לְעוֹלָם, tasim l'olam,
כִּי אַתָּה הוּא ki atah hu
מֶלֶךְ אָדוֹן לְכָל הַשָּׁלוֹם. melech adon l'chol hashalom.
וְטוֹב בְּעֵינֶיךָ לְבָרֵךְ V'tov b'einecha l'vareich
אֶת עַמְּךָ יִשְׂרָאֵל et am'cha Yisra·el
בְּכָל עֵת וּבְכָל שָׁעָה בִּשְׁלוֹמֶךָ. b'chol eit uv'chol sha·ah bishlomecha.

Grant abundant peace to Your people Israel always,
for You are the Sovereign of all peace.
May it be pleasing in Your eyes
to bless Your people Israel
in every season and moment with Your peace.

> During the Ten Days of Repentance:
>
> בְּסֵפֶר חַיִּים, בְּרָכָה וְשָׁלוֹם, B'sefer chayim, b'rachah, v'shalom,
> וּפַרְנָסָה טוֹבָה, נִזָּכֵר וְנִכָּתֵב לְפָנֶיךָ, ufarnasah tova, nizacheir v'nikateiv l'fanecha,
> אֲנַחְנוּ וְכָל עַמְּךָ בֵּית יִשְׂרָאֵל, anachnu v'chol am'cha beit Yisra·el,
> לְחַיִּים טוֹבִים וּלְשָׁלוֹם. l'chayim tovim ulshalom.
>
> In the book of life, blessing, peace, and prosperity,
> may we be remembered and inscribed by You,
> — we and all Your people Israel —
> for a good life and for peace.

בָּרוּךְ אַתָּה, יהוה, הַמְבָרֵךְ Baruch atah, יהוה, hamvareich
אֶת עַמּוֹ יִשְׂרָאֵל בַּשָּׁלוֹם. et amo Yisra·el bashalom.

Blessed are You, יהוה, who blesses Your people Israel with peace.

עֹשֶׂה שָׁלוֹם בִּמְרוֹמָיו, Oseh shalom bimromav,
הוּא יַעֲשֶׂה שָׁלוֹם עָלֵינוּ Hu ya·aseh shalom aleinu
וְעַל כָּל יִשְׂרָאֵל, v'al kol Yisra·el,
וְעַל כָּל יֹשְׁבֵי תֵבֵל, v'al kol yosh'vei teiveil,
וְאִמְרוּ: אָמֵן. v'imru: Amen.

May the One who makes peace in the heavens
make peace for us,
for all Israel, and for all who dwell on earth.
And let us say: Amen.

The Kaddish: A Door

*The Kaddish which follows is the doorway
between the Amidah and our concluding prayers.
Whatever you're feeling in this moment,
bring that into your prayer.*

Kaddish Shaleim

יִתְגַּדַּל וְיִתְקַדַּשׁ שְׁמֵהּ רַבָּא. Yitgadal v'yitkadash, sh'meih raba,
בְּעָלְמָא דִּי בְרָא כִרְעוּתֵהּ, b'alma di v'ra chiruteih, v'yamlich
וְיַמְלִיךְ מַלְכוּתֵהּ malchuteih
בְּחַיֵּיכוֹן וּבְיוֹמֵיכוֹן b'chayeichon uvyomeichon
וּבְחַיֵּי דְכָל בֵּית יִשְׂרָאֵל. uvchayei d'chol beit Yisra·el.
בַּעֲגָלָא וּבִזְמַן קָרִיב וְאִמְרוּ אָמֵן. Ba·agala uvizman kariv; v'imru: **Amen.**

**יְהֵא שְׁמֵהּ רַבָּא מְבָרַךְ Y'hei sh'meih raba m'varach
לְעָלַם וּלְעָלְמֵי עָלְמַיָּא. l'alam ulalmei almaya.**

Magnified and sanctified! Magnified and sanctified! May God's Great Name fill the world God created. May God's splendor be seen in the world in your life, in your days, in the life of all Israel. Quickly and soon! And let us say, Amen.

Forever may the Great Name be blessed!

יִתְבָּרַךְ וְיִשְׁתַּבַּח, Yitbarach v'yishtabach
וְיִתְפָּאַר וְיִתְרוֹמַם וְיִתְנַשֵּׂא v'yitpa·ar v'yit·romam v'yitnasei
וְיִתְהַדָּר וְיִתְעַלֶּה וְיִתְהַלָּל v'yit·hadar v'yitaleh v'yithalal
שְׁמֵהּ דְּקֻדְשָׁא **בְּרִיךְ הוּא** sh'meih d'kudsha **b'rich hu**
לְעֵלָּא מִן כָּל בִּרְכָתָא וְשִׁירָתָא, l'eila min kol birchata v'shirata,
תֻּשְׁבְּחָתָא וְנֶחֱמָתָא, tushb'chata v'nechemata,
דַּאֲמִירָן בְּעָלְמָא וְאִמְרוּ אָמֵן. da·amiran b'alma; v'imru: **Amen.**

Blessed and praised! Splendid and supreme!
May the holy name, Bless God, be praised,
beyond all the blessings and songs, comforts and consolations,
that can be offered in this world.
And let us say: Amen.

תִּתְקַבֵּל צְלוֹתְהוֹן וּבָעוּתְהוֹן   Titkabel tzlot'hon uva·ut'hon
דְּכָל בֵּית יִשְׂרָאֵל   d'chol beit Yisra·el
קֳדָם אֲבוּהוֹן דִּי בִשְׁמַיָּא   kadam avu·hon di bishmaya;
וְאִמְרוּ אָמֵן.   v'imru: **Amen**.

יְהֵא שְׁלָמָא רַבָּא מִן שְׁמַיָּא   Y'hei shlama raba min shmaya
וְחַיִּים עָלֵינוּ וְעַל כָּל יִשְׂרָאֵל,   v'chayim aleinu v'al kol Yisra·el;
וְאִמְרוּ אָמֵן.   v'imru: **Amen**.

עֹשֶׂה שָׁלוֹם בִּמְרוֹמָיו   Oseh shalom bimromav,
הוּא יַעֲשֶׂה שָׁלוֹם   hu ya·aseh shalom,
עָלֵינוּ וְעַל כָּל יִשְׂרָאֵל,   aleinu v'al kol Yisra·el,
וְעַל כָּל יוֹשְׁבֵי תֵבֵל, וְאִמְרוּ אָמֵן   v'al kol yoshvei teiveil; v'imru: **Amen**.

May our prayers, and the prayers of the entire community,
    be accepted before You, our Parent.

May there be peace and life, great peace and life
from heaven above for us and all Israel. And let us say, Amen!

May the One who makes peace in the high heavens
make peace for us, for our whole community, and for all the peoples of the world.
    And let us say: Amen.

151 MAARIV / EVENING PRAYER

What follows is an interpretive / alternative Aleinu. If you would like to daven full-text, you can find the full Aleinu in the morning service on p. 94.

Aleinu: Od Yavo Shalom

Raḥ yiji a-ssalaam	راح يجي السلام	עוֹד יָבֹא	Od yavo shalom
'alaina	علينا	שָׁלוֹם עָלֵינוּ	aleinu
Wa'ala kul il-'aalam.	وعلى كل العلام.	וְעַל כֻּלָּם.	v'al kulam.
Salaam	سلام	שָׁלוֹם	Shalom
'Alaina wa'ala kul	علينا وعلى كل	עָלֵינוּ וְעַל כָּל	aleinu v'al kol
il-'aalam	العالم	הָעוֹלָם	ha·olam
Salaam salaam.	سلام سلام.	שָׁלוֹם שָׁלוֹם.	Shalom shalom.

Peace will yet come to us, to everyone, to the whole world.

כַּכָּתוּב בְּתוֹרָתֶךָ, Kakatuv b'Toratecha:
יהוה יִמְלֹךְ לְעוֹלָם וָעֶד. יהוה yimloch l'olam va·ed.
וְנֶאֱמַר, V'ne·emar:
וְהָיָה יהוה לְמֶלֶךְ עַל כָּל הָאָרֶץ, V'yaha יהוה lemelech al kol ha·aretz,
בַּיּוֹם הַהוּא יִהְיֶה יהוה אֶחָד, bayom hahu yihyeh יהוה echad
וּשְׁמוֹ אֶחָד. ushmo echad.

As it is written in Your Torah:
Adonai will reign forever and ever.
And it is said: On that day Adonai will be God over all the earth,
and on that day God will be One and God's Name will be One.

Mourner's *Kaddish*

יִתְגַּדַּל וְיִתְקַדַּשׁ שְׁמֵהּ רַבָּא. Yitgadal v'yitkadash, sh'meih raba,
בְּעָלְמָא דִּי בְרָא כִרְעוּתֵהּ. b'alma di v'ra chiruteih.
וְיַמְלִיךְ מַלְכוּתֵהּ, V'yamlich malchuteih
בְּחַיֵּיכוֹן וּבְיוֹמֵיכוֹן, b'chayeichon uvyomeichon,
וּבְחַיֵּי דְכָל בֵּית יִשְׂרָאֵל. uvchayei d'chol beit Yisra·el
בַּעֲגָלָא וּבִזְמַן קָרִיב וְאִמְרוּ אָמֵן. ba·agala uvizman kariv; v'imru: **Amen.**

יְהֵא שְׁמֵהּ רַבָּא מְבָרַךְ **Y'hei sh'meih raba m'varach**
לְעָלַם וּלְעָלְמֵי עָלְמַיָּא. **l'alam ul·almei almaya.**

יִתְבָּרַךְ וְיִשְׁתַּבַּח, Yitbarach v'yishtabach,
וְיִתְפָּאַר וְיִתְרוֹמַם וְיִתְנַשֵּׂא v'yitpa·ar v'yit·romam v'yitnasei
וְיִתְהַדָּר וְיִתְעַלֶּה וְיִתְהַלָּל v'yit·hadar v'yitaleh v'yit·halal
שְׁמֵהּ דְּקֻדְשָׁא בְּרִיךְ הוּא sh'meih d'kudsha **b'rich hu**
לְעֵלָּא מִן כָּל בִּרְכָתָא וְשִׁירָתָא, l'eila min kol birchata v'shirata,
תֻּשְׁבְּחָתָא וְנֶחֱמָתָא tushb'chata v'nechemata
דַּאֲמִירָן בְּעָלְמָא, וְאִמְרוּ אָמֵן. da·amiran b'alma; v'imru: Amen.

יְהֵא שְׁלָמָא רַבָּא מִן שְׁמַיָּא Y'hei shlama raba min sh'maya
וְחַיִּים עָלֵינוּ וְעַל כָּל יִשְׂרָאֵל, v'chayim aleinu v'al kol Yisra·el;
וְאִמְרוּ אָמֵן. v'imru: Amen.

עֹשֶׂה שָׁלוֹם בִּמְרוֹמָיו Oseh shalom bimromav,
הוּא יַעֲשֶׂה שָׁלוֹם עָלֵינוּ hu ya·aseh shalom aleinu,
וְעַל כָּל יִשְׂרָאֵל, v'al kol Yisra·el,
וְעַל כָּל יוֹשְׁבֵי תֵבֵל, v'al kol yoshvei teiveil;
וְאִמְרוּ אָמֵן. v'imru: Amen.

MAARIV / EVENING PRAYER

I pray to You God,
that the power residing in Your Great Name
be increased and made sacred
in this world which God created freely
in order to preside in it, and grow its freeing power
and bring about the messianic era.
May this happen during our lifetime
and during the lifetime of all of us
living now, the house of Israel.
May this happen soon, without delay
and by saying AMEN we express agreement and hope, **AMEN.**

**May that immense power residing in God's great name
flow freely into our world and worlds beyond.**

May that Great Name, that sacred energy,
be shaped
and made effective
and be acknowledged
and be given the right honor
and be seen as beautiful
and uplifting
and bring jubilation.
Way beyond our input
of worshipful song and praise
which we express in this world
as our agreement and hope, **AMEN.**

May that endless peace
that heaven can release for us
bring about the good life
for us and for all Israel
as we express our agreement and hope, **AMEN.**

You, who harmonize it all
on the highest planes:
bring harmony and peace to us,
to all Israel and all sentient beings
as we express our agreement and hope, **AMEN.**

(translation: R' Zalman Shachter-Shalomi z"l)

Here and Gone

You're most palpably here
in the moment departure begins.

We turn off the artificial lights,
feel the darkening of the sky.

I'm the deer, caught
in Your presence.

When it grows too dark
we sing without words

and that's what cracks me open.
My cup overflows.

There is nothing but You.
You are everything.

(Rabbi Rachel Barenblat)

Havdalah

הִנֵּה אֵל יְשׁוּעָתִי,   Hineh el y'shu·ati,
אֶבְטַח וְלֹא אֶפְחָד,   evtach v'lo efchad,
כִּי עָזִּי וְזִמְרָת יָהּ,   Ki ozi v'zimrat Yah,
וַיְהִי לִי לִישׁוּעָה.   v'y'hi li l'y'shu·ah.
וּשְׁאַבְתֶּם מַיִם בְּשָׂשׂוֹן   Ushavtem mayyim b'sasson
מִמַּעַיְנֵי הַיְשׁוּעָה.   mimainei hay'shu·ah.

Here is the God of my salvation; I will trust and not be afraid.
For God is my strength and my song, and will be my salvation.
Draw water with joy from the living well, the waters of redemption.

לַיהוה הַיְשׁוּעָה   La-יהוה hay'shu·ah
עַל עַמְּךָ בִרְכָתֶךָ סֶּלָה.   al amcha birchatecha selah.
יהוה צְבָאוֹת עִמָּנוּ מִשְׂגָּב לָנוּ   יהוה tz'vaot imanu misgav lanu
אֱלֹהֵי יַעֲקֹב סֶלָה.   Elohei Ya·akov selah.

Salvation is God's; may Your blessing rest upon your people.
The God of hosts is with us; the God of Jacob protects us.

יהוה צְבָאוֹת   יהוה tz'vaot
אַשְׁרֵי אָדָם בֹּטֵחַ בָּךְ.   ashrei adam bote·ach bach.
יהוה הוֹשִׁיעָה   יהוה hoshi·ah
הַמֶּלֶךְ יַעֲנֵנוּ בְיוֹם קָרְאֵנוּ.   hamelech ya·aneinu b'yom koreinu.

לַיְּהוּדִים הָיְתָה   Layehudim haita
אוֹרָה וְשִׂמְחָה וְשָׂשׂוֹן וִיקָר.   ora v'simchah v'sasson v'ikar,
כֵּן תִּהְיֶה לָּנוּ.   Kein tihyeh lanu.

The God of hosts: happy is the one who trusts in God!
God, save us, You Who will answer us on the day when we call!

"For the Jews there were light, happiness, joy, and honor"
—may we have the same.

כּוֹס יְשׁוּעוֹת אֶשָּׂא,   Kos yeshuot esa,
וּבְשֵׁם יהוה אֶקְרָא.   u'v'shem יהוה ekra.

I raise the cup of salvation, and call out in the name of the One:

Hold up the glass of wine.

בָּרוּךְ אַתָּה יהוה, Baruch atah יהוה,
אֱלֹהֵינוּ מֶלֶךְ הָעוֹלָם, Eloheinu melech ha·olam
בּוֹרֵא פְּרִי הַגָּפֶן. borei p'ri hagafen.

Blessed are You, Adonai our God, sovereign of all worlds,
Who creates the fruit of the vine.

Put down the wine.
Hold up the spices, then pass them around and inhale their sweetness.

בָּרוּךְ אַתָּה יהוה, Baruch atah יהוה,
אֱלֹהֵינוּ מֶלֶךְ הָעוֹלָם, Eloheinu melech ha·olam
בּוֹרֵא מִינֵי בְשָׂמִים. borei minei besamim.

Blessed are You, יהוה our God, source of all being, Who creates various spices.

Hold up the braided candle and see your radiance reflected there.

בָּרוּךְ אַתָּה יהוה, Baruch atah יהוה,
אֱלֹהֵינוּ מֶלֶךְ הָעוֹלָם, Eloheinu melech ha·olam
בּוֹרֵא מְאוֹרֵי הָאֵשׁ. borei m'orey ha·esh.

Blessed are You, יהוה our God, enlivener of all worlds, creator of the light of fire.

בָּרוּךְ אַתָּה יהוה, Baruch atah יהוה,
אֱלֹהֵינוּ מֶלֶךְ הָעוֹלָם, Eloheinu melech ha·olam
הַמַּבְדִּיל בֵּין קֹדֶשׁ לְחוֹל, hamavdil beyn kodesh lechol,
בֵּין אוֹר לְחֹשֶׁךְ, beyn or lechoshech,
בֵּין יִשְׂרָאֵל לָעַמִּים, beyn Yisra·el l'amim,
בֵּין יוֹם הַשְּׁבִיעִי beyn yom hashevi·i
לְשֵׁשֶׁת יְמֵי הַמַּעֲשֶׂה. lesheshet yemey hama·aseh.
בָּרוּךְ אַתָּה יהוה, Baruch atah יהוה,
הַמַּבְדִּיל וּמְגַשֵּׁר בֵּין קֹדֶשׁ לְחוֹל. hamavdil um'gasher beyn kodesh lechol.

Blessed are You, יהוה our God, source of all being,
Who separates between holy and ordinary, between light and dark,
between different communities, between the seventh day and the ordinary week.
A fountain of blessings are You, יהוה,
Who separates and bridges between holy time and ordinary time.

Drink the wine.

Eliahu HaNavi / Miriam HaNeviah

אֵלִיָּֽהוּ הַנָּבִיא,	Eliyahu hanavi,
אֵלִיָּֽהוּ הַתִּשְׁבִּי, אֵלִיָּֽהוּ הַגִּלְעָדִי.	Eliyahu hatishbi, Eliyahu hagiladi.
בִּמְהֵרָה בְיָמֵֽינוּ יָבֹא אֵלֵֽינוּ,	Bimheira beyameinu, yavo eleinu,
עִם מָשִֽׁיחַ בֶּן דָּוִד,	im moshi·ach ben David.
עִם מָשִֽׁיחַ בֶּן דָּוִד.	im moshi·ach ben David.

מִרְיָם הַנְּבִיאָה	Miriam han'vi·ah
עֹז וְזִמְרָה בְיָדָהּ,	oz v'zimrah b'yadah.
מִרְיָם תִּרְקֹד אִתָּֽנוּ	Miriam tirkod itanu
לְהַגְדִּיל זִמְרַת עוֹלָם.	l'hagdil zimrat olam.
מִרְיָם תִּרְקֹד אִתָּֽנוּ	Miriam tirkod itanu
לְתַקֵּן אֶת הָעוֹלָם.	l'taken et ha·olam.
בִּמְהֵרָה בְיָמֵֽנוּ	Bimheirah v'yameinu
הִיא תְבִיאֵֽנוּ אֶל מֵי הַיְשׁוּעָה!	hi t'vi·einu el mei hay'shu·ah.

Elijah, the prophet; Elijiah, the Tishbite; Elijah, the Gileadite!
Come quickly in our days and bring messianic transformation.

Miriam the prophet, strength and song in her hand;
Miriam, dance with us in order to increase the song of the world.
Miriam, dance with us in order to repair the world.
Soon she will bring us to the waters of redemption!

(second verse by Rabbi Leila Gal Berner)

Shavua Tov

שָׁבֽוּעַ טוֹב! Shavua tov!

Shavua tov, a week of peace. May gladness reign, and joy increase!

SOURCES

"Holy Space," Susan Schorr. Printed with permission.
"Meditation on Possibilities," Rabbi Janet Madden. Printed with permission.
"A Prayer in Unlikely Places," Rabbi David Evan Markus. Printed with permission.
Mourner's kaddish translation by Rabbi Zalman Schachter-Shalomi z"l. Reprinted from opensiddur.org.
Hebrew aleph-bet calligraphy by Michel D'Anastasio. *Creative Commons license*
Renewed ashrei, Rabbi Evan Krame. Printed with permission.
"Body Hodu," Rabba Kaya Stern-Kaufman. Printed with permission.
"Give Praise," Rachael Hermann. Printed with permission.
"Nishmat," Rabbi Lewis John Eron. Printed with permission.
"Your Name Be Praised," Rabbi Zalman Schachter-Shalomi z"l. Reprinted from opensiddur.org and *Psalms In A Translation for Praying*, ALEPH 2014.
Chatzi kaddish translation by Rabbi Daniel Brenner. Printed with permission.
"Bar'chu, Dear One," Lev Friedman. Printed with permission.
"Good (Yotzer Or)," Rabbi Rachel Barenblat. First published at Velveteen Rabbi. Reprinted with permission.
"So much (Ahavah Rabbah)," Rabbi Rachel Barenblat. First published at Velveteen Rabbi. Reprinted with permission.
Shema artwork, Donna Tukel. Printed with permission.
"Listen Up, Y'all," Rabbi Rachel Barenblat. First published at Velveteen Rabbi. Reprinted with permission.
"Emet" photograph by Ze'ev Barkan. Creative Commons. Reprinted with permission.
"Journey," Rabbi Jill Hammer. First published in *Siddur HaKohanot*, Hebrew Kohenet Priestess Institute, 2017. Reprinted with permission.
"Open Your Gate," Rabbi David Evan Markus. First appeared in *Chadeish Yameinu*, Temple Beth El of City Island, 2014. Reprinted with permission.
"Blessing for Peace," Mark Nazimova. Printed with permission.
"Waters of Healing," Rabbi Shohama Wiener. Printed with permission.
"Broken-hearted," Shir Yaakov. Appears on the album *Lah*, 2015. Reprinted with permission.
Tree woodcut by Jonathan Gibbs. Reprinted with permission.
Photograph "Mem," by Ze'ev Barkan. Creative Commons, reprinted with permission.
"Kedushat HaYom," Rabbi Janet Madden. Printed with permission.
"Kedushat Keter," Rabbi Rachel Barenblat. Printed with permission.
"Offering (What we do for love)," Jacqui Shine. Printed with permission.
"Tikanta Shabbat," Rabbi Lewis John Eron. Printed with permission.
"Reverse acrostic," Rabbi Jennifer Singer. Printed with permission.

"There is no other," Trisha Arlin. First published in *Place Yourself: Words of Prayer and Intention*, Dimus Parrhesia press, 2018. Reprinted with permission.
Mourner's Kaddish Translation by Rabbi Burt Jacobson. Printed with permission.
"Home," Kohenet Taya Shere. First appeared in SageWoman Magazine Issue #56 / Winter 2001; reprinted with permission.
"The Sunset Prayer / Davvenen Minhah," Jacob Glatstein / Ruth Witman.
"As We Bless," Faith Rogow. Reprinted with permission.
"Evening," Rabbi Rachel Barenblat. First published at Velveteen Rabbi. Reprinted with permission.
"Unending Love," Rabbi Rami Shapiro. Reprinted with permission.
"Redemption," Mark Nazimova. Reprinted with permission.
"I Stand," Mark Nazimova. Printed with permission.
"Prelude to the Amidah," Rabbi David Zaslow. Printed with permission.
"Here and Gone," Rabbi Rachel Barenblat. First published in *Open My Lips*, Ben Yehuda Press 2016. Reprinted with permission.
"Miriam Ha-Neviah," Rabbi Leila Gal Berner. Published at Ritualwell. Reprinted with permission.